THERE'S A HOUSE IN THE LAND
[Where A Band Can Take A Stand]

By SHAUN D. MULLEN

ISBN 1475178409

(c) 2011-2014 by Shaun D. Mullen

Published by Fishy Business Press
All rights are reserved. Except for brief quotations
in a review, this book may not be reproduced in any form
without the permission of the author.

Published in August 2014

Printed in the United States of America

Cover design, farmhouse icon and formatting
by Anja Gudic

Editing by Victoria Digby Whisson and Susan Winters Cook

Title page photograph of Lobelia by the author

Book title adapted from "Nothing's Very Easy When Your Baby's
In The Lake," words by Larry Adams and music
by Snakegrinder & The Shredded Fieldmice

CHAPTER SUBTITLE LYRICS FROM

(Foreword) "Stairway to Heaven"
by Jimmy Page and Robert Plant
(One) "All Along the Watchtower" by Bob Dylan
(Two) "You Are the Eyes of the World"
by Jerry Garcia and Robert Hunter
(Three) "With a Little Help From My Friends"
by John Lennon and Paul McCartney
(Four) "Woodstock" by Joni Mitchell
(Five) "Our House" by Graham Nash
(Six) "Atomic Dog" by George Clinton
(Seven) "Benedictus" by Dave Cousins
(Eight) "Both Sides Now" by Joni Mitchell
(Nine) "Sailin' Shoes" by Lowell George
(Ten) "Jammin'" by Bob Marley
(Eleven) "I Hear You Knockin'"
by Dave Bartholomew and Pearl Kind King
(Twelve) "Don't Bogart Me" by The Fraternity of Man
(Thirteen) "Eight Miles High"
by Gene Clark, Jim McGuinn & David Crosby
(Fourteen) "Winter in America" by Gil Scott-Heron
(Fifteen) "Ol' 55" by Tom Waits
(Sixteen) "Crazy Fingers"
by Jerry Garcia and Robert Hunter
(Seventeen) "Get Out of Denver" by Bob Seger
(Eighteen) "Rocky Mountain High" by John Denver
(Nineteen) "Down In The Florida Keys" by Tom T. Hall
(Afterword) "Into the Mystic" by Van Morrison
(Coda) "Brokedown Palace"
by Jerry Garcia and Robert Hunter

THERE´S A HOUSE IN THE LAND

To Deborah, who showed me what was possible,
fired my imagination, urged me to never give up,
and saw me through to the finish line.

FOREWORD

*"If you listen very hard the tune will come to you at last.
When all are one and one is all to be a rock and not to roll."*

A character in the *Doonesbury* comic strip once called the 1970s "A kidney stone of a decade," and compared to the 1960s and 1980s, it indeed was. It was a period of economic and political decline and, of course, abuses of power with Watergate being the worst but by no means only scandal. Decades get demythologized; it is a quintessential part of the Great American Meat Grinder, but nobody has bothered to demythologize the 1970s because there was nothing mythical about them.

The decade opened with a cyclone killing a half million people in Bangladesh and the Beatles breaking up, at midpoint, the Vietnam War was sputtering to an end and New York City was teetering on the brink of bankruptcy, while its conclusion was marked by the Iran hostage crisis and introduction of the first Sony Walkman. The decade's three presidents -- Nixon, Ford and Carter -- were dirty or mediocre, and the state of the union was not good.

It also was a time of bad hair and bad music, but none of that mattered to the tribe who lived on a farm beyond Philadelphia's far western suburbs. At first glance, this farm would seem to have been one of the then-ubiquitous communes, but it most definitely was not.

There's A House In The Land (Where a Band Can Take a Stand) is the story of that tribe and that farm. It is fact lightly disguised as fiction in that the places, events and people are real, but the names of some places and people have been changed to protect the innocent. As well as the guilty.

-- SHAUN D. MULLEN

THE TRIBE

Ali: Passing through
Bess: Doer
Bigfoot: Techie
Bix: Veteran, raconteur
Caitlin: Pattie's older daughter
Callie: Bartender
Dadd: Glue
Dan: Father of Pattie's children
Davis: Veteran, founder
Denny: Evader
Doctor Doc: Veteran, entomologist
Doctor Duck: Founder, sage
Edward: Singer
Hawk: Veteran, master mechanic
Jack: Veteran, namer of names
Jane: Student
Jena: Pattie's younger daughter
Pattie: Earth mother
Shaun: Veteran
Shell: Explorer
Teana: Free spirit
Vi: Seeker
Zarnie: Adventurer

CHAPTER ONE

*"There must be some way outta here
said the joker to the thief"*

The first time I went out to Kiln Farm, bumping along in an aluminum beach chair anchored to the floor in the back of Eldon's Chevy Step Van, it seemed like it took forever although the farm was only 10 miles from New Park.

Back then New Park was a quaint college town without a single decent restaurant. But it did have the New Park Tavern, which Edgar Allan Poe is said to have cursed when he got falling-down drunk following a lecture at the college and was thrown out, as well as two other establishments where students could hoist a pint before returning to the comfy confines of a picture book campus with ivy-covered buildings. The Poe story is apocryphal because the tavern didn't exist when the poet-storyteller gave the lecture, but that hadn't prevented the management from plastering raven images on beer mugs and T-shirts.

Today that quaintness is long gone. There are several decent restaurants, the tavern is still raven-centric, but has been cleansed of its rusticated piss and beer charm. About the curse, I don't know. After a night of drinking, students now return to a campus that has grown up to become a world-class university known for far more than its football team.

As for the farm, all but the farmhouse was razed years ago. The garden, apiary, barn, milk house, chicken coop, black walnut tree that little Caitlin swung under, and the fields that seemed to go on forever, were bulldozed and replaced by cookie cutter townhouses in a development insultingly called Kiln Farms.

Eldon turned off the state road onto a driveway flanked by row after row of field corn and began the bumpy ascent to a place that would be my home for the next 10 years.

My initial impression was a cosmic *wow!* For the first time since I had returned from Nam, I finally felt like I was home. It just wasn't the kind of home I had expected when a past and future resident of the farm, whom I had met in Saigon shortly before we caught Freedom Birds home, invited me to hang out until I got my bearings.

The upper story of the farmhouse came into view as we began to crest the last hill and broke free of the cornfields. Windows blazing brilliant orange with the reflection of the late afternoon sun framed by white stucco walls and topped by a faded red tin roof created the appearance of a gigantic grinning jack o' lantern. Appropriate, because it was Halloween. There was music playing. Very loud music. I recognized it as King Crimson's "In the Court of the Crimson King."

The music was blaring from large Pioneer speakers on a porch flanked by two guys guarding a half keg of beer in a wash tub filled with chunks of ice. Both could have been mistaken for guitar god Duane Allman with their tall and lean builds, bushy moustaches and long hair, while an Irish setter, whom I imagined had to be deaf from the volume of the music, slept on the steps between the porch and front lawn, where a hotly contested game of horseshoes was being played.

The guy sitting on one side of the keg was resplendent in a sparkling red lamé jumpsuit, *MARS* emblazoned in big letters on the back. His head and arms were painted a matching red, as well. The guy on the other side was wearing a similar only blue lamé jumpsuit with *VENUS* across the back, his head and arms painted blue. Trick or treating had obviously started early for these two planets.

There was a costume party that evening. A hundred or so people filled the lawn, living room and an adjacent room called the stereo room where rock bands from New Park jockeyed for attention.

The party was a blur of grease-painted faces under shock wigs, a couple of people-sized condoms with eye holes, several Richard and Pat Nixons, cross-dressing witches with long, warty noses, a Wolfman and a Batman, and a guy who was dressed as Christopher Columbus and kept whispering "I'm Don Cristobal Colon" in sepulchral undertones as he came and went in a blue fog of marijuana smoke. I felt like a voyeur in an LSD-laced version of Fellini's *La Dolce Vita*, especially when I observed the proceedings through a large, gilt-framed mirror on a living room wall with a couple of cracks that fittingly further distorted reality.

Not being better prepared, I came as myself, although someone did lend me an ill-fitting evening coat with swallow tails. I spent much of the night coping with acid-driven culture shock in the cornfield below the front yard.

The light from a full harvest moon was wondrously bright and seemed to throb as I looked up at the night sky from a sort of fetal position while occasionally massaging a forearm where the heavy wool coat rubbed against the skin. The stereo was now cranking out Pink Floyd's *Ummagumma* album, and I had become so disoriented that had it not been for the *thump-thump-thump* of the speakers and *clink* of the horseshoes, I would have had trouble figuring out where the house was because of the height and maze-like quality of the corn.

The keg, now blown, was floating in melted ice as I made my way onto the porch from the cornfield. The crowd had thinned, while the Irish setter, who was now wearing plastic moose antlers as he snuffled his way through the bacchanal in search of scraps of food, including a partially eaten plate of Swedish meatballs and baked beans balanced on the chest of Christopher Columbus, who had passed out on a living room couch.

I spent my first night at the farm on a mattress in the Phone Booth. This room was off a short hallway connecting the kitchen to the stereo room, had briefly been a darkroom and was now mostly used as a phone booth because the farm's telephone -- a rotary dial job in canary yellow covered with peace symbols and Chiquita Banana stickers -- was in the kitchen and the kitchen was not the place to have a telephone conversation. This inconvenience was addressed by a very long cord.

I didn't sleep much that first night, a combination of the acid and the Phone Booth also being a place to screw during parties, this having dawned on me after the third or fourth tandem of heavy breathers threw open the door and fell onto the mattress, and in one instance, on me.

The farmhouse was vaguely Colonial in architectural style with Georgian flourishes like the twin chimneys on the exterior side aspects, and interior wainscoting, chair rail, crown and other molding. It was what is known as a father-son house. Viewed from the front, the left and right halves were mirror images of each other.

I was to learn that the left half was built of native fieldstone, mostly black granite, in the mid-18th century, while the right half also was of fieldstone and gifted, in all likelihood, by the original farmer, or the farmer's eldest son, to his own eldest son in the early 19th century. The fieldstone ended below the roof line where there were two courses of pinkish Belgian bond bricks artfully laid in opposite directions, which is to say skewed slightly one way on the first course and slightly the opposite way on the second, providing a sort of sawtooth effect. When stuccoing over fieldstone became popular later in the 19th century, the bond bricks were left as is. It had been many years since the stucco had been painted. A few window panes on the second floor and most on the third were made of original -- or at least very old and very thick -- shot glass. These were especially lovely when they frosted over. No shot glass panes had survived on the first floor.

  Behind a porch leading to identical recessed front doors were a living room and stereo room on the father side of the house with frayed oriental area rugs that must have been quite pricey when new, while the floorboards around the rugs -- some as much as a foot in width -- reflected light with a dull but beautiful antique glow. What had been the living room on the son side of the house was being used as a wood shop, which included long work benches, one of them backed by lovely old oak pharmacy shelves stuffed with assorted hand tools and fitments, a table saw and drill press. There also was the Phone Booth, of course, and a big kitchen that had been added on to the rear of the house.

  No one knew where the original kitchen was, but it may have been what was called a summer kitchen and was located in the backyard. This is because traces of the foundation of a smallish, long-ago building would appear near the kitchen addition toward the end of dry summers. A large tin-over-wood front porch and small kitchen porch were added about 1900, probably the same time as the kitchen, judging from the period cinder block used for the porches and kitchen, as well as an identical tin roof of the same vintage atop the farmhouse. The original stone steps were visible if you aimed a flashlight under the front porch boards.

  A front staircase led to the second floor, as well as a narrow and winding back staircase that continued up to the third floor, or attic, its steps worn into parabolic shapes because of the many years of use. The seldom used front staircase led from a small foyer to a second-floor hallway, an unexpected visual treat for visitors.

  A threadbare oriental runner in a green and dusty rose motif ran the length of the hallway. One wall was covered with mirrors of various shapes and sizes in frames painted a rainbow of fun house colors, as were doors to four bedrooms, the bathroom, and the house's only closet of any size. Another wall was covered with Andy Warhol-like wallpaper of race cars. There were also psychedelic teardrops.

  The bathroom was located at the end of the hallway. Its walls, floor and ceiling had been slathered with loudly patterned texture paint -- not exactly what you wanted to see first thing in the morning when you were sitting on the toilet with a hangover. The bathroom smelled of Dr. Bronner's Peppermint Liquid, the soap of choice for discerning hippies of the era, although it turned what little hair I had to the consistency of straw, and was dominated by an enormous claw foot tub and jury-rigged shower. The shower head was attached to a red rubber laboratory hose that would occasionally break loose from its mooring and like a berserk terrorist firing a Kalashnikov on full automatic, soak the walls, floor and ceiling. There was a bull's eye on the back of the toilet seat mocking guys with poor aim, and across from the toilet an ancient wax cylinder dictation machine on wheels, complete with a microphone at the end of a thick cord, under which *Crawdaddy!* and other magazines, Zap Comix, and for many years Stewart Brand's *Whole Earth Catalog*, were stashed for perusal while awaiting nature's call.

The attic was a curious affair. The father side had a large and small bedroom, while the son side was unfinished except for a floor of wide oak boards covered with black paint. This sizable space had become a sort of walk-in closet where the castoffs discarded by former housemates had been dumped. These included a dog-eared copy of Carlos Castenadas' *The Teachings of Don Juan*, which was a sensation on college campuses at the time, a sex toy with corroded batteries, 1950s Philco Predicta television with a swivel picture tube on a pedestal atop a box containing the electronics, a goodly number of psychedelic black light posters, a pair of small brass bells that may have once adorned a Middle Eastern camel saddle, and the kind of horned helmet you might see in a Wagnerian opera.

Early generations at the farm had planted shade trees around the farmhouse, including black walnuts, cherries, oaks, arbor vitae and a cedar that had survived and thrived. With the exception of the cedar, these trees had grown to be taller than the house and were natural air conditioners. They kept us comfortable in all but the hottest weather.

There also were three pear trees and an elderly sassafras tree, identified by a housemate with a botanical bent as having been propagated during the 18th century because its roots were thought to be a cure for gonorrhea. I wondered whether the founder of the farm had the clap.

Heating a large house without a stick of insulation was another matter. There were four fireplaces, but only the one in the stereo room was operable. Two of the farm's first residents had gone back to New Park to wait out the cold weather over the first winter, leaving a third to spend it alone and usually without heat because there never was enough firewood. There was a coal furnace in the cellar that had been converted to oil, but it had seen better days.

The one operable fireplace was not up to the task even when there was plenty of firewood, so the vintage Philco television was traded for a Franklin stove, which was parked on a slab of slate in the kitchen. This stove took small pieces of wood and only a few at that. Many a cold evening my first winter was spent drinking Genesee Cream Ale, sipping cognac, smoking pot and hatcheting logs down to suitable size to generate a feeble amount of heat that barely broke the chill.   That none of us amputated fingers was a wonder.

   We upgraded to an Ashley Automatic wood stove before the following winter -- it cost a mere $165 at a general store in nearby Pennsylvania Dutch country -- and Ben's invention was banished to rust on the kitchen porch. Ashley Automatics are butt-ugly, but their fireboxes are immense and can be top loaded with large chunks of wood, as well as accessed through a front door to remove ashes. This we could do in our sleep, banking the wood to one side, shoveling out ashes from the other side, and then banking again to shovel out the remaining ashes. Through the magic of convection, the Ashley heated most of the house, the first and second floors anyway. During one especially cold winter, it cranked out heat non-stop from late November until mid-March. A cast iron kettle atop the stove customarily bubbled with a potpourri of cinnamon sticks, nutmeg and sometimes apple slices that wafted through the kitchen and up the back stairs.

Nothing warms better than wood. Nothing.
When you heat with wood you are warmed thrice, first while cutting it, then while splitting it, and finally while burning it. Mundane methods of heating like oil, gas and electricity barely warm your skin. Wood heat insinuates itself into walls, floors and your very bones. There was a certain perverse pleasure in padding around in stocking feet in the depths of winter although the banshee was howling. We knew that friends in their much newer New Park digs were not nearly as comfortable.

With the arrival of the Ashley came the first major weapons in an arsenal of sledges, wedges, axes, saws and eventually a couple of Stihl chainsaws that wedged, axed and chainsawed their way through a woodlot filled with piles of downed branches and the occasional storm-felled tree, as well as several pick-up truck loads of firewood gifted during the course of a year by a tree surgeon friend. After a couple of heating seasons, we had established a routine: Faster burning black walnut, ash and box elder were tossed into the Ashley's cavernous maw in late fall, slower burning white and red oak, cherry and apple in the winter, then black walnut, ash and box elder again in early spring.

Osage orange -- or what we called monkey ball trees as kids -- lined one side of the shorter of the two driveways. These trees, among the densest native woods, had been planted many years earlier as a wind and snow break, but their overhanging branches got in the way as farm machinery grew larger, and had to be cut back. Osage orange, which took twice as long as oak to dry because of its density, was the wood of choice on the coldest of nights because of the extraordinary amount of heat it threw off as it burned.

   I stuck it out in the Phone Booth for a few days and then asked whether I could move into the unfinished half of the attic. That was okay, so I set to work removing the black paint from the floor with a big disk sander, considerable elbow grease and the lubricating properties of Genesee Cream Ale.

   The original floor also had marvelously wild boards and gradually reappeared as the paint disappeared. After several coats of a light stain and polyurethane, it looked beautiful. A housemate and I lugged up an antique Chippendale-style chest of drawers and gilded gold mirror that had belonged to a grandmother, a coffee table lifted from a dormitory lounge at the university, and double bed mattress. There wouldn't have been enough room for a box spring even if we could have muscled one up the narrow back stairway because the attic ceiling sloped dramatically. The walls at each end were barely four feet high.

Two housemates and I came upon a smallish barn that was on the verge of collapse. We stripped much of its lovely weathered wood siding with the owner's permission, and that became a wall dividing the attic into two large rooms connected by a scavenged door on which I hung the brass bells, which would tinkle when the door was opened. I insulated the ceiling on both sides of the wall, which was the only insulation the house would ever have, nailed siding to the rafters, and with the leftovers built a floor-to-ceiling bookshelf on the side where my bed was. I never got around to finishing the other side. It eventually reverted to being a dumping ground.

I was to record my thoughts over the decade in a series of small artist sketch books. The initial entries in these journals of a sort were ponderous and written painstakingly with a pricey Rapidograph technical pen. I eventually realized that this was stupid; I obviously had composed these entries as if someone was looking over my shoulder, or conscious that someday someone might read and stand in judgment of them. I finally let my hair down, such as it was, and began writing more candid if fleeting thoughts in an ordinary fine point felt-tip marker, ballpoint pen or whatever else other than a pencil might be handy.

My first night in the attic was blessedly restful. Nam had its own sounds and smells, some of them not pleasant, while the motel in New Park where I had stayed was so noisy and cigarette smoke saturated that I couldn't sleep. I was laboring over my inaugural journal entry when I was interrupted by Percy, the farm's peacock, who heralded the dawn from an upper branch of the arbor vitae outside my lair with a repertoire of high-decibel sounds that I soon got used to and eventually became rather fond of. It was kind of like living next to a railroad track, yet barely noticing when a train rattled by. Percy was a terrific watchbird, ripping off a foghorn-like sound when there were interlopers so deep and loud you might have thought an ocean liner was approaching.

The second night was likewise restful until I woke before dawn and Percy and heard the faint thrum of a car motor. A few minutes later, there was still a thrumming, and I got up to investigate. It seemed that a housemate had fallen asleep at the wheel of his VW Beetle after driving home following a night of tippling at the New Park Tavern. He was also in the habit of falling asleep on the toilet.

The third night was only a few hours old when Percy let loose with his ocean liner riff, accentuated with *Psycho* soundtrack-like shrieks, in response to a bullhorn-amplified voice announcing that the house was surrounded. I jumped up and hit my head on the ceiling.

"This is the F.B.I.," the voice declared. "We know you're harboring a Marine absent without leave. Tell her to come out immediately and no one will get hurt."

"Her" was Jo Lynne, a willful naïve and skinny sprout of a woman who had a faded sort of beauty although she was only 20 or so. She had indeed gone AWOL from a Marine base in North Carolina, in fact for the second time, hitchhiked north instead of south to her hometown as she had the first time, and learned in New Park about the haven that the farm had become. She showed up a few days before the Halloween party with what she said were all her worldly possessions in a duffel bag.

Jo Lynne explained that she was from a genteel fifth-generation Alabama family. She was stood up at her senior prom and in a fit of rebellious anger went downtown to enlist in the Marines the next day. "I thought I wanted to be a dancer, but I couldn't do it. I thought I wanted to be a Marine, but I couldn't do it," she told me in the course of our first and only conversation of any substance. It was as though we were longtime intimates. "I thought I wanted to be a lesbian, but I couldn't do it. I'm no good at anything I try to do." It was hard to disagree with her.

Jo Lynne was last seen leaving the Halloween party on the back of a Harley Davidson with a biker and never came back for her duffel bag.

No, Kiln Farm wasn't the kind of home I had expected.

CHAPTER TWO

*"Wake up to find out that you are the eyes of the world
but the heart has its beaches its homeland
and thoughts of its own"*

The small town parochialism of New Park had gotten to the farm's founding fathers, Doctor Duck and Davis. They went looking for a party house in the not-too-distant countryside and Kiln Farm was exactly what they wanted.

Never mind that the house was an unheated wreck. Bart, Doctor Duck's Irish setter, could run to his heart's content, the barn was suitable for working on cars and trucks, and there was no one living within a quarter of a mile or so. It was September 1969, and the rent paid a banker on Philadelphia's Main Line, a son of the farm's last residents, who were said to have decamped in the 1950s, was $200 a month.

The farm was at the edge of the far western Philadelphia suburbs, and after being razed for townhouses became the far western suburbs. In geological terms, it was situated on the Piedmont Plateau, which lies between the Atlantic coastal plain and Appalachian Mountains, a region characterized by low rolling hills and the southeastern-most of a series of parallel ridges so evident when you look at a relief map of Pennsylvania.

  Underlying this region is an extraordinary conglomeration of rock formations. These include the black granite that was the primary component of the fieldstone in the farmhouse walls, as well as Cockeysville marble, a limestone interlayered with schist which acts like a giant water-retaining sponge. As a result, the water table remained relatively high even when the farm's surface soil dried up during droughts. The soil elsewhere in the Piedmont is poor, for the most part, primarily in the South where soil-robbing tobacco and cotton are the primary crops, but the soil on and around the farm was rich in nutrients despite being shot through with clay.

  The farm itself was 160 or so acres of mostly tillable land with a small woods, two creeks and two driveways that bisected a more or less rectangular property. The land rose to a high point where the house was situated. If the house was at the center of a clock face, a chicken coop was in a 1 o'clock direction, a barn with two silos and a milk house at 4 o'clock, a two-story shed at 7 o'clock, and what was to become a garden at 9 o'clock. We later built a stable and loafing pen in a field above the chicken coop, a pig sty and shelter above the garden, and another loafing pen below the shed.

The longer of the two driveways wound up to the house from the state road, while the shorter one led to a township road. The longer driveway had a swale on a nearly 90-degree turn at its halfway point dominated by an immense sycamore. The turn got little sun in the summer and reliably froze over from runoff from an underground spring in the winter. Neither driveway was paved, and the longer of the two eventually became so deeply rutted that it was impassable.

Twenty-five or so people called the farm home in the 10 years I lived there, not counting hangers on. There were eight people when I moved in, including Doctor Duck, who had worn the red lamé jumpsuit, and Davis, who I had met in Saigon and had worn the blue jumpsuit at the Halloween Party. There were two people when I left, and our comings, as well as our goings, were mostly dictated by happenstance. I moved in because I needed a place to stay, others because they liked what they saw and decided to stay, some because they were escaping unhappy relationships, and a few others who lived in

New Park most of the time and were willing to pay rent to have a country crash pad.

Four housemates left this mortal coil before their time.

Pattie and little Caitlin, the older of her two daughters, perished when Dan, the father of the children, lost control of his station wagon on the rain-slicked state road not far from the farm and T-boned a charter oak, so designated because it dated back to Colonial times. Caitlin was three years old. Jena, not quite two, suffered a broken arm and leg. No one had been seat belted, and although Pattie had been gifted a baby seat at a shower while pregnant with Jena, it was not being used. Dan walked away physically uninjured although deeply damaged psychologically.

Doctor Duck's fondness for Genesee Cream Ale and then Rolling Rock beer eventually packed in his liver, but it was Edward who departed in the most spectacular manner. He was high and tried to flag down a freight train outside the New Park Tavern while standing on the tracks.

Doctor Duck, whose tall, thin frame became more bloated by the year, his once kempt long brown hair scragglier, fingernails grosser because of infrequent bathing and once clear blue-grey eyes usually bloodshot, eventually moved back to New Park for good so he could devote more time to drinking himself to death while polishing his alter ego as the bumptious Doctor Duck, which of course was not his real name. Many people had no idea what his real name was.

He would begin his day with breakfast at a greasy spoon where he always ordered two slices of bacon, two pieces of toasted white bread with butter, and a cup of tea with a splash of milk and two teaspoons of sugar. That regimen eventually gave way to a diet pretty much consisting of beer, with the occasional Sunday dinner at the farm his only real sustenance. As the tavern's part-time maintenance man, sometime carpenter who built booths for the back room and a new sign that he hung from above the front porch, and full time ID-checking doorman at night, he would crack his first Rolling Rock about 8 in the morning after hosing down the rubber mats behind the tavern's townie and college bars, and then drank through to last call. Paid in part in beer, he spent much of each day on a captain's chair at the corner of the townie bar where he dispensed pearls of wisdom such as:

We're all brothers and sisters on the surface of the Planet Earth.

> *Don't get a tattoo. It's bad to poke holes in your spacesuit.*

As well as the ever serviceable:

> *There's no such thing as a longest and shortest day of the year. They're all 24 hours.*

September was Doctor Duck's favorite month because that was when the university reopened and there would be a new freshman class of coeds whose backsides he would ogle from the front porch of the tavern as they streamed by. It was my favorite month because of the endless days of sunshine, low humidity and cool evenings. I went on the road often, but never in September.

Four housemates and I were Nam veterans and one just a vet. Dadd and Bigfoot had not served in the military because they drew high numbers in the draft lottery. I don't recall Edward's circumstances, while Doctor Duck got a medical discharge after he was banged up in a motorcycle accident after Army basic training. This was not well known because he sought to create the impression he had served in the war without ever coming right out and saying so. He put Disabled Veteran license plates on his car although he had been 13,000 miles away from the action.

Dadd spent a summer sleeping on the living room couch after graduating from the university in New Park, and took over the bedroom used by Zarnie, who had painted the second floor hallway in that riot of colors, when he decamped to Colorado.

Dadd had an immutableness about him that changed little in all the years I have known him, although I suspect he had been a bit of a bully in his jock days -- he was a varsity wrestler at the university -- that the farm bled out of him. He hadn't seen the inside of a barber shop in years, wearing his brown hair long and beard, which obscured a deeply dimpled chin, even longer. He had an infectious laugh that masked a certain sternness, twinkly brown eyes, and did even the most difficult crossword puzzles in pen.

Dadd majored in accounting, but his true love was farming although he had grown up in a split-level house in a suburban housing development. In this he had a considerable asset -- a solid grasp of plant and animal genetics. As our garden grew, he was able to ascertain the symbiotic relationships that certain plants have with other plants. In the case of tomatoes, he interspersed them with basil to keep predatory insects at bay, which they did. He could sex chicken hatchlings, determining which were females and destined to be egg layers and which were males and destined to go away, and understood the breeding cycles of dairy animals.

  Everything about Bigfoot, and not just his size 14 shoes, was large. He had an automaton-like walk, and our cats fled as he approached them. He was not particularly coordinated, and if there was a rock anywhere near him, he would stub a toe on it. In bad weather, he would wear two olive drab Army parkas snapped together that made him look like a pine tree. He was the only one among us who wore glasses, had a crew cut and didn't have a moustache or beard, merely a bit of peach fuzz on his chin, which set him apart from the rest of the guys. He was also the only one among us who smoked cigarettes.

  Bigfoot was a bit of a boffin -- a brainy laboratory technician who had an interest in computers early on. Hence his alternate nickname of Captain IBM. He had a deep voice, bottomless pit of a stomach, and could put away enormous amounts of food and beer. The conclusion of meals were accentuated by loud and sonorous belches, for which Pattie would remonstrate him, prompting an even louder and more sonorous series of belches, then laughter all around. He also farted a lot, and had a predilection for dozing off on the toilet, among other places.

Bigfoot's older brother was my first friend when my family moved to New Park. I was 11 years old. We went to high school together, but I had lost track of him until, exploring the second floor of the farmhouse on my first day there, I opened the door to Bigfoot's bedroom and saw his brother napping. He stirred and opened his eyes.

"Oh, it's you, Moon," he said, using the nickname he had given me after Moon Mullins, a then popular newspaper comic strip. "Good to see that you and Davis made it home."

Edward was tallish, burly and broad shouldered, had blue eyes, a ruddy complexion, and a long blonde ponytail which kind of made him look like Allman Brothers band organist-vocalist Gregg Allman, as opposed to Doctor Duck and Davis, who both looked like Gregg's brother Duane. He was a construction worker by day and the lead singer of what could be called the farm's house band -- Snakegrinder and the Shredded Field Mice -- which sometimes rehearsed in the stereo room because of complaints from neighbors when they practiced in the basements of friends' homes in New Park. Edward carried a little leather harmonica case with him like an Englishman would carry an umbrella, was a not bad player and terrific blues singer; I thought his rendition of the Rolling Stones' "Wild

Horses" was better than the Mick Jagger original.

He was the kind of guy who did not seem destined to die in bed of old age, and so it was. Despite a tough-guy exterior, he would rather walk around a bug than step on it. On the night of his death, he pulled two hapless university students from their stalled car on the railroad tracks outside the New Park Tavern as a Chesapeake & Ohio freight train pulling dozens of boxcars bore down on the crossing. Edward had a head full of Quaaludes, a then trendy sedative-hypnotic barbiturate that was said to heighten sexual pleasure, but put me to sleep. Anyhow, he tried to flag down the freight while standing on the tracks. The train won. The Poe Curse, I suppose.

Jack, the first of the Nam veterans, was built like a football linebacker, which he had been in high school. He had what later became known as a unibrow, thick eyebrows joined across the bridge of his nose, although that did not mar his good looks. He was of medium height but seemed to be low to the ground, while his broad shoulders and ample biceps betrayed an almost inhuman strength. I once saw him lift the back bumper of his girlfriend Vi's VW Beetle in the parking lot behind the tavern, the back wheels spinning furiously as she revved the engine and tried to drive away. This was during a time when, as Jack put it, "we were finding cohabitation to be stressful."

He had obsidian eyes, and a dark brown beard and hair that although fairly short was in his face much of the time. He would wear a T-shirt on his head when he sweated, giving him the appearance of a wimpled woman from medieval times. He, like me, was left-handed, and like me would rather get lost than ask for directions.

Jack had been a Marine infantryman who was awarded a Bronze Star and two Purple Hearts, one for a Viet Cong bullet that grazed his right ear and another that had taken out a piece of his left shoulder. He was offered a battlefield promotion from sergeant to second lieutenant, which he proudly refused. He seldom talked about the heavy shit he had been through.

Doctor Doc, who had the botanical bent and pointed out the sassafras tree, was tall and solidly built. His hazel eyes had an incorporeal look, which probably was a result of him being nearsighted and refusing to wear glasses. Unlike most of the guys, he got frequent haircuts. His hair and moustache were prematurely gray, and his moustache resembled barbed wire for the first few days after he would periodically shave it off and grow it back. He was partial to flannel shirts and white tube socks, and had good manners that seemed to come naturally, as opposed to an Eddie Haskell-esque obsequiousness ("That's a lovely dress you're wearing, Mrs. Cleaver") some of us turned on like a light switch when we needed to make nice. He was genuinely humble and foreswore obscenity, "double damn" being about as blue as he got.

Doc got great pleasure from using archaic expressions. For example, when someone was goofing off, and there was plenty of that, he would say they were "skylarking." He answered questions in the affirmative not with "yes" but "aye-aye," was an autodidact and fluent in Latin, which he would summon at unexpected times, although the phrases he used were sometimes cumbrous to my ear and I had taken four years of Latin in high school. He also knew some Greek and Sanskrit, was a backgammon master, and insatiably curious. This led him to take things apart he could not always put back together, including his International Harvester pickup truck, which spent as much time on cinder blocks in the barn as on the road.

Doc had been a Navy petty officer medic assigned to a Marine Corps battalion. He came home with a Bronze Star, blown out eardrums and a lingering case of malaria, and also seldom talked about the heavy shit.

Davis, after living at the farm a while, enlisted in the Army before he could be drafted and became a warrant officer and the pilot of a lethally-armed Cobra helicopter gunship. He was known by his surname, perhaps because his given name was Llewellyn, or so I recall, and had earned a Bronze Star and two Air Medals when I met him as our tours were ending, the latter honors given sparingly and only for flying many -- well, too many -- combat missions. He never talked about the heavy shit.

Tall and thin, Davis had deep blue eyes, favored a British commando sweater blown out at the elbows, and was as quiet as his bosom buddy Doctor Duck was voluble. A casual observer might mistake that the fact he seldom spoke as a kind of lassitude, but friends knew his pauses between words spoke louder than the words themselves. I never heard him raise his voice, even in a noisy place like the townie bar. He was on a quest to figure out who he was, which after he left the farm for good led him into Eckancar, a quasi-religion that embraces soul travel. That in turn led him to another kind of travel as a navigator on TWA jumbo jets.

Baxter, or Bix as Jack nicknamed him, was on the short side, stocky and was also partial to flannels. He had an infectious *tee-hee* of a pianissimo laugh, brown eyes, was a decent stand-up bass player, something of a pinball wizard and card sharp, had a big heart and was always willing to do a friend a favor as long as it didn't involve lending money. His knees usually ached, he claimed from standing for hours ladling out gourmet Army fare on chow lines, and he went through Tiger Balm like some people go through chewing gum. It was a sure sign that a big change in the weather was imminent when Bix was especially achy.

He was later transferred from a mess hall to a motor pool where as a lowly private first class he drove an ammunition truck for the duration of his tour, something he seemed to never stop talking about.

If you need to know, I am a college dropout, tall, have a widow's peak and was already losing my light brown hair in high school, which made me the go-to underage poseur for buying beer. I have a moustache and beard that I began to grow the day I arrived back in the States. My mother's woman friends thought me handsome and remarked on my deep blue eyes. My accomplishments, such as they were, included giving my high school graduation speech ("Freedom Is Not Free") because the valedictorian had been busted for bringing grain alcohol-injected oranges on our senior trip to New York City, and knowing a little bit about everything and nothing about anything.

I made sergeant in the Army and *never* talked about my experiences because I was fortunate to be Chairborne in

Saigon, as opposed to Airborne in Upcountry, and didn't fire a single shot in anger. In fact, I never was issued a weapon. Nor do they give Purple Hearts for busting open knees while breaking up bar fights.

Then there was Hawkeye, he of greenish-brown eyes, freckled face, long red hair and, for many years, a long beard, all of which gave him a sort of Red Beard the Pirate countenance. I never heard him say a bad thing about another person, he was and remains deeply generous, and his smile has lit up many a room.

He was so nicknamed not because of the character in M*A*S*H, a television sitcom that did not debut until a couple of years after he moved to the farm, but because of his visual acuity as a sergeant first class scout instructor at the Army Special Forces school in the jungles of the Panama Canal Zone. Hawk, as we called him, was too valuable to be sent to Nam, but his students were sent there in droves. He once told me he knew the Army let him live so that others could be killed.

Except for Bix, Nam was not discussed. It usually was

studiously ignored. This was a consequence of the long-running horror show in which battlefield relationships were precarious because friends had a way of ending up dead or maimed. Flowing from this was a paradoxical guilt among survivors, myself included, because we had somehow made it out in one piece. The university in New Park would have never been confused with antiwar hotbeds of the era like Columbia, Berkeley or Ann Arbor, and a consequence was that returning veterans did not encounter much of a backlash. No one was called a baby killer, although Davis, who was wearing a field jacket stripped of insignia, was heckled by a couple of college students one evening as he walked down the town's main drag with Edward, who lifted the most vocal of the guys by his lapels and deposited him in a trash can outside the bus station.

When the last chopper lifted off the roof of the American embassy in Saigon in April 1975, bringing that awful war to an ignominious end, no one mentioned it around the kitchen table although it was very much on everyone's mind. Later that night, somebody did approach Davis in the townie bar and inquired as to whether he was glad the war was over. Davis glared at the guy.

"I didn't know there was a war," he replied as he turned heel and walked away. I followed him out into the parking lot. There were tears in his eyes.

CHAPTER THREE

*"Oh I get by with a little help from my friends,
Mmm, I get high with a little help from my friends,
Mmm, I'm gonna try with a little help from my friends"*

After moving to Kiln Farm, Jack started a construction business with Denny, who briefly was a housemate. They specialized in post-and-beam horse barns, the farm happened to be in horse country, and there were plenty of well-heeled people who could afford them.

Denny was a few pounds south of slender and somewhat bandy-legged, of medium height with long sandy blond hair, and had lenticular eye sockets that gave him a feral yet not unhandsome appearance. He favored an Australian drover's coat and outback hat in cold weather, and was the heaviest drinker among us no matter the season, with a predilection for payday bourbon binges. These resulted in a couple of drunk driving arrests, as well as close encounters with immovable objects, sometimes when I happened to be a passenger in his work truck. As a draft dodger, Denny was a fugitive until President Carter pardoned him and hundreds of thousands of other young men in 1977. It was an aftershock that didn't begin to redress the immorality of a war that discriminated against the poor, protected the well-to-do who had the resources to avoid becoming cannon fodder, and sought to imprison the conscientious.

  Doctor Doc enrolled in the doctoral program in entomology at the university's agriculture college in North Park on the GI Bill, where he specialized in apiary science. That's beekeeping and such.

  From a single hive hard by the the garden, Doc built up the farm's apiary, and within a couple of years there were a dozen hives and his bees were producing honey by the gallon from feasting on fruit trees and vegetable plants as the garden grew and expanded. Because of his deafness, Doc would have to be shaken awake when the postmaster of the closest post office, in fact its only employee, would call in a panic at 7 in the morning to inform us that a shipment of bees had arrived by Parcel Post, and would Mister Doc kindly please pick them up as soon as possible thank you.

  Bix got a job as a welder at a shipyard and fancied himself a shade tree mechanic. He specialized in repairing two-stroke Saabs. Or "Saab Stories," as Jack called them.

Hawk operated heavy equipment for a construction company and plowed snow in the winter. If there was an Olympic event for the backhoe, he would have been a gold medal winner. Unemployed, I accepted his invitation to work with him one winter and was assigned my own dump truck fitted with a plow and loaded with salt. Although bracketed between snow-heavy winters, there wasn't so much as a flurry.

After returning to the farm, Davis like me had drifted around, but eventually fell into doing leather work with Doctor Duck. Had Doctor Duck been a printer, I suppose Davis would have been a printer's devil. In the years before Doctor Duck climbed all the way into the bottle, he turned out beautiful embroidered belts and wallets, as well as gear -- holsters, bandoliers and such -- for the New Park Police in a little shop called The New World Trading Company across the railroad tracks from the New Park Tavern and hard by a funeral home where, as Dr. Duck put it, they threw "going-away parties."

The shop, more familiarly known as the Duck Shop, was redolent with the smell of leather and oils, and in cold weather, the occasional unwashed homeless person sleeping under a workbench. I enjoyed hanging out there, and would watch he and Davis cut, stitch and finish leather. Doctor Duck had sewn those lamé Halloween jumpsuits and tailored a satin-lined suede vest for a girlfriend without taking a single measurement. It fit her like a glove.

Doctor Duck was a master at getting the most useable material from a cowhide with the least amount of waste, and expert at running the cut pieces through a foot treadle-powered industrial sewing machine to stitch them together. Hell, he was a master at everything he put his mind to. Including becoming an acute alcoholic.

Doctor Duck's sole business failure was running a submarine sandwich shop with Davis in a storefront around the corner from the leather shop. They called the shop Munchies, and it featured whole wheat sub rolls, which they assumed would be a big hit with the hippy-dippy college crowd, students from the university's newly opened North Campus, as well as free delivery anywhere in New Park.

As anyone knows who grew up in the Mid-Atlantic, the heartland of the great Italian sub, the key is the roll, typically semolina with hard crust and soft innards, but Munchies' whole wheat rolls were dense and tasted like old wallets. Or so I imagined.

Free delivery lasted only two or three nights because the driver, an elfin ex-con by the name of Angel, lost his shit and put a fist through a wall in an apartment lobby when a customer asked him to break a hundred dollar bill. The customer called the police. Recognizing Angel as a friend of Doctor Duck, that strange but okay fellow who made their leather uniform gear, they sent him on his way with a warning.

Doctor Duck never got a ticket for parking his cars in front of the Duck Shop facing the wrong way, which he did quite intentionally, and the shop was a no-police zone. The police were well aware that there was a procession of people from the townie bar at the tavern who strolled over to smoke copious quantities of pot many an evening. They couldn't have missed the clouds of telltale smoke rolling out of the front door, across the porch and onto the sidewalk, but nevertheless looked the other way.

Munchies closed after about a week, what modest profits there were having been eaten by the help.

Pattie was a tall beauty with long, dark brown hair and penetrating blue eyes who dressed, spoke and lived simply. She had a streak of romanticism as well as a gentle *je ne sais quoi* about her. I imagined Pattie to look like Lady Rowena, the Saxon beauty in Sir Walter Scott's *Ivanhoe*. Beyond jeans and flannel or T-shirts, depending upon the season, she had but a couple of blue denim dresses, or at least I never saw any others, although she did have a buckskin outfit, moccasins and a headdress she wore when dressing like an Indian on Halloween. She never wore makeup except for face paint on Halloween. Her years at the farm milking goats and doing other chores took a toll on her hands, but she seldom used lotions or salves. There was a world weariness about her that dissolved only after she would crack open an after-dinner beer, her cares dissolving into smiles as she would absent-mindedly curl a lock of hair with a finger and tuck it behind an ear, only to fall back in her face moments later.

There were six other woman housemates when I moved in, and in subsequent years.

Jane was the baby of our family and a few years younger than the rest of us. She was an undergraduate at the university, had Katharine Hepburn good looks, light brown hair that she wore short, green eyes and a sweet smile that barely masked an innocence that was the polar opposite of Pattie's world weariness. Jane had an interest in feminist literature that she tried to spark in me after she moved into the attic. (No, dear, I never did get through Djuna Barnes' *Nightwood*; dog knows I tried.) She also had a green thumb, and with Doc built cold frames from old storm doors that enabled us to start seedlings for the garden even when there was still snow on the ground.

Michelle -- or Shell, as she liked to be called -- was tiny, weighing perhaps 90 pounds, had deep brown eyes, porcelain skin and an enormous Harpo Marx-ish corona of curly black hair she tied back in a bun more or less held in place with tortoiseshell swallow-tail brooches. She had a spiritual side and a deep soulfulness, but was a natural-born comic who could cross her eyes and make fish lips at the same time, as well as being a terrific cook, although stray strands of her unruly hair sometimes found their way into the food she prepared. I had known Shell since we met at a Christmas party when we were in high school, and aside from my mother she had been the only one to write to me while I was in Nam. Shell was in love with Hawkeye, whose name she pronounced *Hawk* (brief pause) *eye* with a throaty bedroom growl. She chased him to Colorado and back to the farm, but he did not give in to her for several years.

Teana and Vi had been friends since they were children. Growing up, they used to joke -- actually, they were somewhat serious -- that they wished their parents would divorce because Teana didn't get along with her mother and Vi with her father. They fantasized that

Teana's father would then marry Vi's mother so they could be real sisters.

Teana was living with Zarnie when I moved in, and she returned to the farm several times through the decade from far flung travels. Tallish, thin and perpetually tanned, she had liquid brown eyes, curly hair and a quick wit. She was passionate about gardening, an interest first sparked at the farm, and went on to get a degree in horticulture.

Vi, a vivacious brunette with piercing blue-gray eyes, blew up the engine of her purple VW Beetle, which was just about her only possession after she left her husband. She bumped into Jack, Hawk and Bix in the townie bar and mentioned her plight in passing. They retrieved the Beetle from the shoulder of a country road and towed it to the farm, where they rebuilt the engine, admonished her to not forget to check the oil, and sent her on her way. Mindblown at the generosity of these strangers, she drove back out to the farm for visits, soon moved into the small attic bedroom across from my lair, and later moved downstairs where she and Jack shared a room.

There also were Ali and Callie, who was introduced to the farm by Jane after they took classes together at the university. Their similarity in names was coincidental. Ali put in a brief appearance in the middle of the decade while Callie arrived on the scene a couple of years before I moved on.

Zarnie was one of those people who looked 10 years younger when he wore a hat over his balding pate. He was of middling height with longish brown hair and a moustache and beard when he didn't feel like shaving, which he usually did not. There was a focus, yet lightness, about him, and he had always had a faraway gaze in his eyes. This was because he was looking West. Zarnie found the farm too confining and informed Teana that he was departing for the wide open spaces of Colorado, although not with her. Teana's was not the last heart he would break.

The farm certainly was not remote. A hot shower was only a short drive away in New Park if the pipes froze, which they did many winters. Yet there still was the exhilarating feeling of being out in the middle of nowhere, at least in the early years before the suburbs commenced their unstoppable march on us. As well as a validation that we had created something special, although no one said as much.

It hadn't occurred to me until I read a book about time that nobody seemed to mind when the clock in the kitchen wasn't replaced for several months after it died. Perhaps we were not unlike the French philosopher Rousseau, who it was remarked didn't begin truly living until he threw away his watch. It's not that time didn't fly or crawl, be relentless, or do any of the many other things time does. It just didn't particularly seem to matter to us. There was so-so radio reception and no television until later in the decade, while the telephone sometimes went unanswered, typically during the marathon backgammon games we played before the arrival of that first television. All of this enhanced the feeling of remoteness.

The book explained there are two kinds of time -- linear time and cyclical time. We exist in linear time. We are born, we live and eventually we die. Yet life is full of repetition. Every day we brush our teeth, eat, urinate and defecate. This is cyclical time, and as my years at the farm piled up, it was this kind of time of which I became acutely, if nevertheless subconsciously, aware. This was because of the farm's lodestone -- the garden -- which without giving a second thought we planted in the spring, cultivated in the summer as the sun grew stronger and the days longer, harvested in the fall and let lay fallow in the winter when the sun had faded and the days shortened, only to again begin the cycle the following spring.

Back then, we were oblivious to a third kind of time -- digital time -- a wave that was yet to break on the shore. My brother, who graduated with a masters degree in something called computer science from the university, had told me of its supposed awesomeness years before it became the coin of the realm.

Most everybody, I suppose, had their roles, and among Jack's was being a namer of names. He gave everyday things pet names. Breaded shrimp were "cocoons." Televisions were "electronic cannons." Food stores were "stupidmarkets." When someone died, they "swallowed their birth certificate." Cola beverages were "carbonated carcinogens," and in all the years that I have known Jack, I have never seen him take so much as a sip of one.

Bix's nickname was Jack's creation. Shell was into yoga and Satchananda, a yogi she hung out with for a time in her search for a path to getting in touch with a higher being, who seemed more interested in fleecing his flock than taking it to higher planes of consciousness. Jack derisively called him Snatchabanana behind her back. I was Captain Cab because of all the chauffeuring I did in my VW bus. Then there were visitors on whom Jack did not shower affection. These included a marijuana hog who would say, "Let's smoke a bone," whom he named

Boner; a woman by the name of Val who had a downer habit whom he named Valium; a woman who constantly yammered whom he named Piper; a guy who bragged about the size of his penis whom he named Johnson; a well meaning fella by the name of Harley whom he named Hardly, and an obnoxious drunk by the name of Suzy whom he named Suzy Creamcheese after the character in the Frank Zappa song.

Jack was barely getting by as a carpenter. Quoting Ishmael in *Moby Dick*, my copy of which he happened to be reading at the time, he decided "to sail about a little and see the watery part of the world," and joined the crew of an ocean-going tugboat that towed trains of petroleum barges from Bayonne, New Jersey to the Carolinas and back. The money was great, but the captain was a bad drunk.

Several voyages on, the tug was caught in a Nor'easter off Virginia as it deadheaded back to New Jersey. Jack said the winds were so ferocious that the train of empty barges started coming around on the tug and threatened to crash into and sink it. The captain had passed out, so Jack and the rest of the white-knuckled crew took turns at the wheel until the storm abated.

"I'm in Bayonne, Captain Cab, and I need you to fucking pick me up," Jack bellowed into the kitchen phone after making landfall. He later said he never believed in the power of prayer, not even in Nam, before this close encounter.

I nicknamed him Ahab and later Moby Jack after his ordeal, but neither stuck. I just didn't have the naming knack.

I can count on one hand the number of times I was alone at the farm. One of those times was unfortunately unforgettable. While climbing a ladder to the loft in the shed to fetch storm windows, a rung gave way and I did a backward swan dive about 15 feet to the floor, landing with a thud and within inches of the rusted carcass of a motorcycle. The breath was momentarily knocked out of me.

I looked up and tried to focus on the shed's rafters while figuring out what to do. I had to act quickly because my back was going to lock up, so I got up and duck walked across the driveway and into the house. I laid down on the mattress in the Phone Booth, where my back did indeed lock up. Shell eventually showed up and came to my aid, which was a favor returned of a sort because only a few days earlier I had come home when *she* had been alone to find her trapped, straightjacket like, in a baggy sweater that had gotten caught on the brooch clamped to her prodigious head of hair, pinning her arms over the head.

Shell drove me to an acupuncturist, a specialty with which I had become kind of familiar in Nam, but was then a rare find Stateside. He helped ease, if not totally eliminate the pain.

Not that any of us had given the provenance of the farm's name much thought, but I figured it had something to do with kilns that baked kaolin, which is a clay-like mineral used in making ceramics. Such kilns had once dotted the area, and perhaps there had been one on the farm.

The real story was unexpectedly revealed when we had a yard sale to get rid of all the stuff people left behind in the attic when they moved on. Little was sold except the psychedelic black light posters. They were a huge hit at 50 cents apiece and still a hit when the price was doubled to a dollar. The horned Wagnerian helmet didn't sell even after being marked down, but was later put to hilarious use.

A goodly number of locals, having an excuse to see what the heck was going on up at the old farm, showed up to gawk. These included identical twin sisters in their eighties, one a retired teacher and the other a retired librarian, who had worked at the high school up the township road.

It was through these two chatty souls that Hawk and I learned more local history in a half hour than I was able to absorb in my entire decade at the farm.

The sisters explained -- one sometimes finishing a thought the other had started -- that the farm was on the northern edge of a large tract of land sold in 1683 by Chief Kekelappen of the Lenni Lenape tribe to William Penn, the great champion of democracy and religious freedom who had founded the Province of Pennsylvania. The land on which the farm was built was called Pamachapuka by the tribe, that being their word for a glacial erratic, a rock different from the rock native to the area. Which in this case rolled in, so to speak, at the end of the last Ice Age. Indeed, there was a large rock in the pasture below the barn fitting that description, only part of which protruded iceberg tip-like from the ground. This rock had been a spiritual lodestar for the Lenni Lenape until settlers drove them away.

The area was already fairly well developed, which is to say substantially deforested and under cultivation, when Old Man Van der Killen, who was said to be a retired sea captain with a peg leg, took deed to the property after migrating from Holland in 1750 and shortening his surname to Kiln.

Our conversation took place in the shade of the gonorrhea-curing sassafras tree, and I found myself again wondering at what exotic port of call the Old Man had been infected.

CHAPTER FOUR

*"We are stardust, we are golden,
we are billion year old carbon,
And we got to get ourselves back to the garden"*

When Doctor Duck and Davis moved to Kiln Farm, there was an impenetrable jungle of multi-flora rose, thistle, pig weed and Johnson grass that began about 30 feet from the kitchen side of the house and extended 300 or so feet to the upper edge of the property. I note by name each of these noxious plants -- termed "fuds" by Jack, as opposed to "buds," which were beneficial plants and animals -- because all are among the most difficult plants to exterminate in the weed world. Some are illegal to propagate in much of the United States. So is marijuana, but more about that later.

Doctor Duck and Davis had about as much interest in gardening as they did in crocheting, so for the first year or so the jungle continued to grow unchecked.
Then Bess and Bunny arrived, although not together.

Bess, a diminutive woman with blond hair and luminous blue eyes who walked with a slight limp from a childhood bout with polio, was escaping an unhappy relationship, in her case the abusive father of her young son and daughter. A city girl wise in many things, but not the wonders of nature, she fell in love with the farm after she met Doctor Duck, who told her she and her children were welcome to move in.

Zarnie had built an earthen and rock dam on the creek below the cornfield across from the front porch. "This is the most wonderful thing!" Bess exclaimed as he pointed out the various fuds and buds, including the flourishing reeds he planted behind the dam. The resulting wetland had become a habitat for wading birds.

Bess and her children lived in the unfinished half of the attic that I was to occupy. Like the war veterans, the farm became a refuge for them, providing stability during a troubling interlude in their lives.

Bess, in the relatively short time she lived at the farm before moving on and into a relationship with a wonderful man who would become her lifelong soul mate, was able to provide the woman's touch the farm so sorely lacked. Nothing as extreme as curtains, but she did start what grew to be a lovely houseplant jungle on the front porch. This included spider plants, begonias, dracaena, schefflera, croton, Boston ferns,

Christmas cactus and a jade, with the musical accompaniment of wind chimes she hung from a rafter. These plants were brought into the living room each autumn, livening up an otherwise drab space thanks to a southern exposure that bathed the room in sunlight. The jade plant was so massive after repeated repottings that it became too heavy to move outdoors and eventually filled a big window well in the stereo room.

With the help of Bunny, Bess also made the initial inroads into a jungle that would become a very special garden.

Bunny was a black, brown and white Nubian goat with enormous drooping ears and sad eyes that did not betray mischievousness, a defining characteristic of goats. She was a castoff from a hippie farm where interest in raising animals had been short-lived. Within weeks of her arrival, Bunny had cleared a small corner of the jungle. The result was a cultivatable patch of earth about 15 feet by 30 feet that Bess laboriously turned with a shovel and hoe. The initial harvest included snow peas, most of which were eaten before they made it to the kitchen, and some peppers and corn.

Over the next several years, a garden of about 30,000 square feet -- the length of a football field and about a third of the width of one -- effloresced, having grow larger and larger spring after spring from its modest beginnings.

All things being equal, the earth gives back what you put into it, and our garden became an organic wonderland.

After trial-and-error experimenting, this was realized by broadcasting ashes from the wood stove and shit from the chicken coop in the winter, plowing the ashes and shit under in the spring, and applying a dusting of agricultural lime before the first seedlings went in. When gifted a cooler of freshly caught sea trout, Doctor Doc buried their nutrient rich heads to disintegrate in and fertilize the then fallow garden, but the dogs sniffed out and dug up every single one. They reeked of fish heads for days.

Snow peas, cabbage and kale started in the cold frames went in first, usually by Saint Patrick's Day. Next came root plants, including carrots, onions, garlic, spuds, yams, beets and mangels for the chickens. With the danger of frost passed, in went peppers, including red and green bells, bananas, Hungarian wax, poblanos, chilis and habañeros, the latter so hot that the only reason we continued to grow them was to flummox boastful visitors, often bikers, who claimed there wasn't a pepper they couldn't handle. A few nibbles on a habañero or a dip of a forefinger into a jar of my habañero sauce would have a biker crying into his leathers.

  There also were various lettuces, broccoli and cauliflower, spinach, eggplants, cukes, zukes, pumpkins, asparagus, rhubarb, peas and lots of tomatoes (but never cherry tomatoes, which Dad thought were a waste of space; I had to agree), yellow and white corn for eating and Indian corn for autumnal decorations. Herbs included sweet basil, coriander, thyme, oregano, parsley and rosemary. Then there were the horseradish roots Hawk dug up in September and ran through a blender after evacuating the kitchen and donning an Army gas mask.

  Our harvests eventually became so large that the bookshelf behind the kitchen table would groan under the weight of canned vegetables, while the milk house freezers were filled with pesto, peppers and shucked corn. There was nothing quite like an envigorating taste of summer in the dead of winter.

  The location in the garden of each kind of vegetable didn't vary much from year to year with the exception of corn, which robs soil of nutrients and doesn't give anything back. We would plant corn in the upper part of the garden one year and the lower part the next. We sowed orchard grass -- a winter-hardy perennial that tolerates just about any weather condition, including drought -- where corn had grown the previous year, and tilled it under after it matured to give the soil a boost.

There also was a red raspberry patch, while huge black raspberries grew along the treeline next to the short driveway. That treeline included mulberry trees that dropped their savory fruit onto old bedsheets we laid down in late spring to capture them for Pattie's rhubarb and mulberry pies.

We planted alternating rows in the garden with annual flowers, primarily marigolds and zinnias. And sunflowers, as well. Sunflowers were not just pleasing to the eye, but an attraction for Doctor Doc's bees, while Percy feasted on the seeds after the sunflowers grew to 15 or so feet tall, wilted, bowed their top-heavy heads and succumbed to gravity.

Most of us pitched in with the tilling, weeded when it was wet and watered when it was dry, but there was the occasional misfire.

Shell, who never got along particularly well with Dadd, thought she might insinuate herself into his stern graces by planting more basil in the flower beds flanking each side of the front porch.

She proudly showed off her handiwork when purple shoots began peeking through the soil.

"Holy crap!" was Dadd's response as a look of bruised dismay crossed Shell's face.

"You've planted ornamental basil, for Chrissakes. It's inedible."

Then there was the pumpkin debacle.

Teana and Vi thought there was money to be made in growing and selling pumpkins, and we planted two rows which produced a bumper crop one fall. The pumpkins -- perhaps 300 future jack o' lanterns in all -- were lugged to the front porch, where they dried, and because Teana and Vi inconveniently moved on, were neglected and eventually rotted into the floorboards.

My contributions to the garden were practical and aesthetic.

I hung a wooden restaurant kitchen door with a porthole at a side entrance bought at an auction, and built an outhouse from barn siding. I situated this *toilette alfresco* in a spot with a sweeping view of the garden. It was on skids and would be dragged to another location when the hole beneath it filled up, or treatments with lime would no longer suppress the odor. There also was a "sculpture," actually a sort of weather vane, I fabricated out of a truck exhaust pipe with a bicycle wheel atop it that was adorned with streamers of various colors. I planted this construction next to the main entrance to the garden where the wheel would turn in the wind to pleasing and welcoming effect.

From Percy and Bunny, our menagerie eventually grew to include a fair number of goats, a bull, pigs, chickens, ducks, geese, guinea fowl, and a horse.

We raised a succession of pigs who arrived in the spring as piglets so small they could fit comfortably in our laps on the ride home from an auction. The pigs were fattened over the course of a summer to 200 pounds or so and then on a fall day be given a last supper of beer. They would be wrestled down, flipped onto their backs, which was a two- or three-person job for we city slickers, and their legs hogtied with bailing twine, their anguished screams making me ponder whether I should become a vegetarian. Which I eventually sort of did. The pigs returned from a butcher a few days later wrapped in kraft paper packages containing spare ribs, hams, bacon and scrapple, which is a regional breakfast dish consisting of a mush of pig innard scraps and trimmings made with corn meal, flour and spices. Our last pigs were named Bert and Ernie for the *Sesame Street* characters, but they were anything but lovable. Despite considerable efforts to keep them penned, they endlessly found ways to get out and wreak havoc in the garden. Bert and Ernie went to the butcher's a few weeks early.

The bull, whom Bigfoot bought and named Bruno, was too much for us and our fences to manage, so we gifted him to a neighboring farmer. It was not be to the last time that Bigfoot and this beast would make meaningful eye contact.

Early on, our chickens were breeds with topknots and exotic plumage that looked cool, but they weren't particularly good egg layers. Under Dadd's guidance, we gravitated to hardier breeds like Barred Rocks, Buff Orpingtons and Rhode Island Reds. We collected about five dozen eggs a day at the chickens' laying peak in summer, most of which went to a natural food co-op in New Park. The proceeds went to a beer keg fund.

We started out with mail-order Khaki Campbell ducks because, like the exotic chickens, they looked cool, but eventually gravitated to Muscovys, a large and seriously ugly breed that hiss but does not quack, fly short distances low to the ground, and are prolific egg layers. Their largish, thick-shelled green eggs were excellent for baking. The mortality rate for ducklings was high with a red fox sometimes gobbling up as many as 20 of the yellow balls of fluff on a summer night like so many hors d'oeuvres. Those that did mature were terrific free-range foragers who kept the wood tick population in check.

  Then there was the pair of Toulouse geese we were gifted. They were magnificent creatures with large dewlaps, brilliant orange beaks and slate gray and snow white feathers, and were much too big for foxes to tangle with. Our pair loved bathing in puddles after rainstorms, ecstatically honk-honking as they did a sort of square dance. The female laid enormous brown eggs with brown spots that were also excellent for baking. We sometimes gave these to an elderly woman of our acquaintance who nostalgically recalled the days when a huckster in a horse-drawn cart sold goose eggs. Alas, the female was in the habit of waddling up to small children at parties and biting their backsides. Rather than break up these mates for life, we eventually gave both of them away.

  Guineafowl sort of resemble partridges, but have featherless heads and black plumage with white polka dots. Ours traveled in packs and resembled mobsters, their Tommy guns tucked under their wings. They would break into hysterical calls sounding like *buckwheat-buckwheat* whenever they encountered humans. Day in and day out, it was as if they had never seen any of us before.

Even with the foxes, the Muscovy population threatened to spiral out of control during breeding season. This we tried to check through periodic roundups we called duck rodeos.

These happenings involved several people, sometimes hapless visitors whom we enlisted, herding ducks into ever tighter circles, or at least that was the objective, where we would try to grab and throw them into feed bags. This high comedy typically took place after smoking pot and drinking beer. There were more misses than hits as ducks would slither out of our grasp and avoid the reaper for the time being. A few of us were armed with poultry hooks. These were long metal rods with wooden handles on one end and hooks on the other. Dadd, Jack and Pattie became pretty good at snaring Muscovys, sometimes even in mid-flight with deft overhand grabs.

Other than Bruno, our only outright failure involved turkeys.

While Percy seemed to be able to utilize every cell of his pea brain and lived long because of an innate street smartness, turkeys are extraordinarily stupid. So stupid that our only hatchlings, confined to a grassy area proscribed with the corrugated metal sides of a child's swimming pool, perished in an August downpour. This was because, and we had read of such instances, they looked skyward with open beaks and drowned.

If there was an official farm flower, it would have been the daylily. The name of this perennial -- also called the tiger lily -- is an allusion to its brilliant orange flowers, which typically last no more than a day, opening in early morning and withering during the night, to be replaced by another flower on the same stalk the next day.

Bess, and later Pattie, split and transplanted daylilies and bearded irises they rescued from the sides of country lanes before the highway department would lay noxious carpets of herbicides that killed everything.

These went into the ground on the southeast side of the house around the corner from the front porch. A few days before our annual party in mid-June and extending into mid-summer, this swath was a riot of purple, yellow, white and orange. Neither daylilies or bearded iris are suitable for cutting and bringing indoors, where they soon wilt. That was very much in keeping with the esthetic sense the farm nurtured. Their beauty belonged in the natural world and not in ours.

Pattie planted variegated hosta, tiny purple Japanese irises, red and pink cosmos and cystopteris (berry) ferns on both sides of the front porch steps. The ferns grew to be immense, and had to be split every other spring or so, while the cosmos didn't winter over and had to be replanted. This I did each spring in her memory. She also planted calla lilies at the top of the long driveway near the kitchen that threw up distinctive and long-blooming pig's ear flowers. They not only outlived her, but came up every spring despite suffering serial deprivations, including being driven over by Doc on several occasions when his pickup truck became stuck in reverse, and accidentally mowed when they were first peeping through the ground early one spring.

My other contributions to this color cavalcade were red, pink and white impatiens and columbines with their from-outer-space dark blue blossoms. I cultivated these flowers in a tractor tire under a pear tree across the side yard from the kitchen. I also planted bee balm and butterfly bush along a snow fence for bees and hummingbirds to feast on.

  Then there was honeysuckle, a flowering vine that was ubiquitous along hedgerows bordering the garden and beneath the osage orange trees along the short driveway. While honeysuckle technically was a fud in the bud-fud continuum, the sweet scent of its flowers perfumed the air from late spring well into the summer, and we allowed it to grow undisturbed.

  There were three elderly pear trees, all neglected and beset with gnarly dead growth. With the help of Hack, a tree surgeon friend, they were given a thorough trimming. The following spring, flowers appeared, the bees had at them, and there was a modest crop of bosc pears with their distinctive long necks and russeted skins in the autumn, and larger harvests in subsequent years. The pears were delicious eaten fresh or in pies.

  The octogenarian sisters said there were 100 or so farms within a couple of miles of ours at the beginning of the 20th century. By the time we took our turn, that number had diminished to about 20. The fields of most of the remaining farms, like ours, were worked by farmers who, as one of the sisters put it, were equipment rich and land poor. Two brothers rented our fields, as well as several others, from the absentee owner and would bring in their cultivating, planting and harvesting equipment each year.

Many of these farms died because small-scale farming, once the backbone of American agriculture, became less viable because farmers' children became less inclined to follow in their parents' footsteps. The big city beckoned. In 1900, there were 5.7 million farms in the U.S. with an average acreage of a bit under 150. By 2000, there were only 2.4 million farms with 460 acres the norm. That number obscures the existence of immense million-acre corporate factory farms that grow the vegetables too few of the obese citizens of our fast food nation eat, as well as the beef and pork they overeat.

George I. was a third or fourth generation farmer (he went back and forth on the number) with a modest spread a couple of miles from our place. Well into his 80s or 90s (he went back and forth on his age, as well), this widower could no longer work his few dozen acres, his children had moved away, and his barn was about to fall down. It was this barn that Jack, Doc and I had stripped of much of its siding for my attic lair. Once tall and muscular, George I. was now stooped to practically a hunchback's posture because his chronic sciatica had never been treated. He had the long and delicate hands less of a farmer than of a pianist, which he had been before arthritis took over.

George I.'s sons wanted to cash in by selling the farm to a developer, while his daughter, who lived in a faraway city, wanted to hold out but seemed to have no interest in helping her father do so with dignity. Meanwhile, George I.'s fieldstone house was in terrible shape. He would joke that he had driven himself the long way around to poverty and lived in a single junk-filled room, used an outhouse because the plumbing had long ago stopped working, and subsisted on boxed and canned food because there was no electricity and hence no refrigeration.

George I. became a frequent guest at Sunday dinners. He said he had served with the American Expeditionary Force in France and Belgium during World War I, and never ran out of stories, some told over and over with different embellishments, usually concerning one mademoiselle or another whom he had met in Gay Paree while playing piano in one bistro or another while on leave, including one woman whom he cracked "had been banged more than a screen door." Beyond the bluster, he imparted a low-key wisdom nourished by his love of the land. He was a shameless if harmless flirt when it came to woman housemates, and would drop and *ratatat* click his upper dentures when he was being especially silly. None of my housemates minded, some flirted back, and all doted on him like a sweet if goofy uncle.

   Hawk bought a double-wide house trailer at an auction, towed it to George I's farm and wired it for electricity. Dadd contacted a social worker who enrolled George I. in a public assistance program, signed him up for food stamps, as well as looked in on him. He lived out the decade on his farm in relative comfort, but his mind eventually packed in and he went to a county-run nursing home. Beyond occasional visits from Hawk, he died very much alone.

   The centerpiece of a farm is the barn. Ours was a faded beauty on the cusp between surviving and falling down.

   A barn is only as stable as its roof and some of the slates had blown off the windward side during the years that ours languished. The inevitable water damage to rafters, other timbers and floors was well under way when we came on the scene. The expense notwithstanding, the slates had to be replaced if the barn was to survive. This arduous and dangerous task, which involved lugging heavy slates up a ladder and then balancing on a steeply-pitched roof to nail them down, was first done by Zarnie and later by Dan.

The barn had been built for a commercial milk cow operation and was large even by the standards of barns in the area. It had five levels crafted from native oak over a fieldstone foundation. The back was open at ground level where there was a loafing pen. There also were stalls and rusting steel milking stations on a whitewashed concrete aisle on the ground level.

The rafters on the first level were barely six feet off the floor. Van der Killens and other 18th century folk seldom reached that height, while the accumulated buildup of hay left no headroom for someone as tall as myself. I continuously -- and I mean for years and years -- bashed my head if I forgot to wear a hat.

The second level was accessed through two massive pairs of doors atop earth ramps where tractors, hay wagons and other farm equipment had once been stored. The bay behind the doors nearest to the farmhouse had a block-and-tackle apparatus for pulling engines, and the remnants of a machine shop. This we used to work on the farm's fleet. The third through fifth levels were lofts with portcullis-like trap doors for bringing up and dropping down hay bales. I loved climbing to the vertiginous top level, opening a door and stepping aside as swallows flooded past me like bats out of a cave.

There was a one-story cinder block milk house built into the east side of the barn. It had been used to process milk in years past and still contained a large stainless steel chilling tank. Two silos constructed of dark brown fired clay blocks, one silo slightly taller than the other, were on the west side. The taller silo had lost its conical steel cap. Both had been used to store corn and grain. Despite having been long empty, they still smelled of both.

The first part of the barn had been built by the descendants of Old Man Van der Killen and probably dated to the early 19th century. There were no signs of the original circa 1750s structure, which might have been demolished or built over when the newer and far larger barn and various additions went up. I do know, because the octogenarian sisters said as much, that the farm's milk was taken by horse-drawn and later tractor-drawn wagon to a railroad siding in the nearest town where milk cans were loaded aboard milk run trains -- yes, that is where the term derives from -- that would take the milk and a few passengers to the city, return with the empties, and load up all over again the next morning.

I was eventually able to identify the oldest section of the newer barn. This is because the timbers were pegged and not nailed, and there were vestiges of an oak peg ladder stair and several tree crotch hooks for hanging gear, as well as what I surmised had been a primitive wooden string latch. All were vestiges of the early 19th century and bespoke a time when barn carpentry was still crude. The newer sections of the barn had hand-hewn nails, while the newest section had machined nails, which did not become widely available until the latter part of the 19th century.

Although we stored hay for the goats in the lowest loft, the barn was substantially empty. Both barn and silos were superb acoustic echo chambers, providing deep and somewhat spooky resonances to harmonizing voices at drunken singalongs and to Blue's flute. He was a wanderer who would pass through from time to time for a meal, after which he would serenade us with marvelous melodies.

Like I said, all but the farmhouse was bulldozed. When I screwed up the courage to pay a visit after being away for many years, there were cookie cutter vinyl-sided townhouses where that magnificent barn had stood. Soccer Mom vans were parked in front of each.

CHAPTER FIVE

*"Our house is a very, very fine house
with two cats in the yard"*

Ours was a very, very fine if unusual house. If there were ever just two cats in the yard, that had to have been back in the beginning.

Despite unceasing efforts to neuter and spay, there were upwards of a dozen cats roaming around Kiln Farm at a given time; too many were castoffs abandoned at the ends of the driveways. The downside to this rolling population explosion were fights among competing males and the money spent on cat food and veterinarian's bills for patch-ups after the fur flew. The upside was that we never had a rodent problem although farms are magnets for vermin.

All the cats were nameless. Then there was Terrapin.

A six-week-old-or-so descendent of cats at the Ernest Hemingway House in Key West, he had been adopted on one of our sojourns to the Florida Keys. Papa, as Hemingway was called by family and friends, had included a provision in his will that the cats living on the grounds of the big house on Whitehead Street were to be cared for in perpetuity. He had said nothing about their not being adopted.

Terrapin, a slightly cross-eyed ball of black and white fluff, was polydactyl as a result of interbreeding. He had six toes on one front paw, five on the other and the usual four on each of his back paws. He made the trip to the farm in the back of my VW bus with only a single upchuck before we had reached the Florida mainland, and was a trouper from there on out.

Percy had no time for the other fowl, let alone four-legged creatures and we humans. But he and Terrapin got on famously. Perhaps they had been pals in previous lives. Terrapin would march back and forth across the yard after him as if he were an aide de camp to a battlefield commander. Percy, as peacocks are, was extremely vain. He would spend hours looking at his reflection in the chrome bumper and hubcaps of the carcass of a 1950s era GMC pickup with Terrapin batting at his magnificent tail when he fanned out his blue-green feathers with distinctive eyes.

Cats are curious critters, but Terrapin was especially so. He liked to ride around on our shoulders, I suppose so that he would have a better view of things, and while Dadd was not especially enamored of cats, Terrapin rode on his shoulders as well.

He was the only cat allowed in the house and would get closed in bedrooms and occasionally in the washing machine, but his meow was so soft -- more like a delicate *mewp mewp* -- that he was unable to call attention to himself. (His purr was, if anything, even softer, more of a vibration than a sound.)

I once opened the door to the closet in the second-floor hallway to be startled by Terrapin jumping onto my shoulder from the top shelf. He regularly fell into and had to scramble out of the rainwater barrels around the house. He would also climb through the open windows of the cars of visitors and sometimes fall asleep, only to be discovered after they had returned home. He disappeared for good one day, probably after he had climbed into a delivery truck and was driven off to new adventures and things about which to be curious.

Although Bunny had long ago been milked out, the idea of having dairy goats because of their nutritious, low-fat milk and the cheese that could be made from the milk, struck the fancies of Dadd and Pattie. After all, there was already a milk house, loafing pen, stalls and haylofts from that long-ago dairy cow operation. And goats loved to feast on the fuds that grew in abundance around the farm.

We eventually had 10 or so milkers -- white Swiss Saanens, brown and white Toggenburgs, and Nubians like Bunny. We entered Lobelia and a daughter, Ophelia, in county fair competitions over two summers, and they came away with first and second place ribbons both times in the Saanen division. These we proudly hung on the kitchen cork board.

The milking operation lost money. There were vet's bills, the rolled oats the girls munched on while being milked, the endless bales of hay they ingested, and the fact that we charged a modest dollar for a gallon of milk. No matter. The goats offered us an opportunity to learn about animal husbandry, including how to maintain the sanitary conditions needed for milking, trimming their hooves, burning the beginnings of horns off kid goats' heads, and an unpleasant chore that had most of the guys suddenly remembering they needed to be somewhere else -- castrating young males.

Like I said, goats have a built-in mischievousness, and my favorite girl, Lobelia, had that in spades. I wanted to name her Kekelappen, or KeKe for short, after the Lenni Lenape chief who had lorded over the land on which the farm was built, but that was vetoed. Instead, she was named Lobelia. I admit this was much better.

Lobes, as we called her, was a milk-producing machine who, if you squinted just so, looked like a bovine Ho Chi Minh with her angular face and long goatee. She would gaze at you with the eyes all goats have in common -- horizontally rectangular pupils sitting amid very pale irises. Lobes gave the impression that she was looking not at, but through you. If she were sizing someone up, she would slightly tilt her head as she chewed her cud and ruminated on whether they were a fud or a bud.

For reasons I was unable to fully fathom, except perhaps that I had a larger version of a goatee, I was a bud. Lobes loved for me to scratch her back and smooch her snout. She would return the favor by nibbling on my beard, but she never pulled it. She had the sweetest breath -- an attar of oats and hay.

Pattie, Dadd, Teana, Vi and I, and later Callie, never had any problem milking Lobes. This was something that did not extend to Shell, Bix and a few other wannabe milkers whom she would torment by waiting until they were almost finished, when she would spectacularly ruin the take. This involved either sticking a rear hoof into the bucket or punting the bucket across the milk house floor. Or both if she were feeling especially mischievous.

   Lobes didn't care for children in general and loud children in particular. I happened to be down in the stable area of the barn during a party when Pattie opened Lobes' stall for a friend's young son.

   "Mommy! Mommy! I'm petting the nice goat!" he shrieked.

   Lobes lowered her head and butted the little dear about three feet in the air.

   When we were children, my brother and I would recite the Lillian Moore ditty about fireflies as we sat on the back steps of our parents' house on summer evenings:

> *If you catch a firefly and keep it in a jar*
> *You may find that you have lost a tiny star*
> *If you let it go then, back into the night*
> *You may see it once again star bright.*

   Those firefly displays of the 1950s never seemed to be replicated in later years, but after I moved to the farm and the previous summer had been especially wet, sheets of fireflies -- and I'm talking about many thousands -- would put on extraordinary displays below the front porch. Their flashes would be so bright that the field and leafy backdrop of trees were illuminated with an amazing luminescence, while on moonless nights their flashes magically melded into the stars in the sky above. The soundtrack to these spectaculars were symphonies of crickets, bullfrogs and sometimes cicadas.

  Animals are great to be around, and you are especially fortunate if you can ride them. Ride some of us did on Dude, who Dad bought for Pattie, realizing her childhood dream of having a horse.

  We built a modest-sized stable with a loafing pen and hay loft in a pasture above the chicken coop that became Dude's domain. This mild-mannered retired thoroughbred was a chestnut gelding with a red-yellow mane, tail and legs, with a splotch of white on his snout. Early on, Pattie rode him along the hedgerows almost every day, usually with the dogs tagging along, and I sometimes imagined her to be Sir Walter Scott's Lady Rowena and the dogs to be from the kennel of her protector, Cedric of Saxon.

  With the birth of little Caitlin, and later Jena, Pattie's rides became less frequent.

The farm's day sounds were a symphony of rooster *cockadoodle dos*, duck *hiss-hisses*, goose *honk-honks*, guineafowl *buckwheat-buckwheats*, Percy's repertoire and Dude's subdued nickerings, goat *maahs*, dog *woofs* and the occasional rasping *kree-eee-ar* of a red-tailed hawk, more commonly known as a chicken hawk. By comparison, the sounds we made were mundane.

At night, the wild critters took over, stealthy and silent except for a never seen owl who would serenade a mate from the treetops. There were white-tailed deer who would have feasted on the garden were it not for the ever watchful dogs who kept that from happening. There also were woodchucks, raccoons, skunks, squirrels, rabbits, chipmunks, mice, voles, toads, frogs, spring peepers, the occasional muskrat, as well as various snakes and salamanders. Among the turtle species were bog or Muhlenberg's turtles, with a distinctive diamond on their heads, pale yellow in color when they are youngsters and increasingly orange as they grow older. I know of one bog turtle who lived to be 50 or so. That species was endangered then and remain so today because of shrinking habitat.

There also were reports of a bobcat in the area and occasional sightings of its paw prints, scat and telltale scratch marks on tree trunks, but no one ever actually saw this elusive beast.

Red foxes and dragonflies held a particular fascination for me.

Other than inattentive motorists and the occasional pissed-off farmer, foxes have no enemies. They figure prominently in folklore, of course, and were characters in Beatrix Potter's *The Tale of Mr. Tod* and other books my mother read to me as a child. Foxes are elusive. This fed my fascination, and I considered seeing one -- whether crossing a road early in the morning, or transiting a field during the day -- to be good luck.

We spotted a mother fox with four kits in a hollow tucked into a field off the long driveway one spring and observed their routine through binoculars. The mother would hunt for the kits, no doubt sometimes bringing home our ducklings and the occasional chicken who was too dumb to return to the coop in the evening, and she would be constantly watchful as her young frolicked outside their den. I am also fortunate enough to have seen two silver foxes, magnificent and rare creatures that are actually mottled black with streaks of silver.

Dragonflies are among the most ancient creatures, some 200 million years older than dinosaurs, and I have observed their mating dance almost every summer of my life.

I was fascinated by this dance as a youngster, although I didn't understand that it was about making baby dragonflies. My brother and I would trap lightning bugs in Mason jars to sell to the man at the agricultural station. He paid us a dime a jar for his research into what made their tails glow, but had we ever been asked we would never considered trapping dragonflies for any amount of money, because they occupied a special place in our young world.

Dragonflies colonize around unpolluted creeks and ponds and were welcome companions when we would go for a soak. They would sometimes alight on our foreheads – even in mating tandems -- if we sat still.

Bats get a bad rap. The little browns who appeared at dusk in warmer weather and flew hither and thither around the yard were most welcome. While the fowl took care of many a wood tick, the bats vacuumed up mosquitoes and other insect fuds with abandon. They would occasionally fly down one of the chimneys and into the house where they would flap around until gently trapped in a bath towel and released outside.

There were dozens of bird species, including hawks and kestrels. A pair of kestrels, which are the smallest North American raptor, nested in a mulberry tree on the short driveway in the spring and became so accustomed to us that we and the dogs could walk within a few feet of them while fetching the newspaper in the morning. Among the birds were omnipresent black crows, whom I sensed knew what was going on better than we did, as well as neo-tropical species that would spend spring and summer in our midst before returning to Central and South America. These included barn swallows, thrushes, waxwings, grosbeaks, flycatchers, and ruby-throated hummingbirds.

  A pair of Baltimore orioles built their species' distinctive nest -- a tightly woven pouch of twigs and straw -- in the upper branches of the black walnut tree under which little Caitlin would swing, while cattle egrets, great white herons and green herons waded in the wetland behind Zarnie's dam.

  Then there were monarchs and tiger swallowtails, among other butterflies. Many of our migrating bird friends would return each spring, but the monarchs that flitted over the garden and fields each summer would never be seen again, their yearly migration of thousands of miles a sort of relay race with females laying eggs for the next generation during their long travels.

Goats can clear cut a pasture in a matter of days, so we rotated our herd from a pasture below the barn to a pasture behind the chicken house, and later to a fairly large pasture off the long driveway. These we wired with a single strand of electric fence. I never saw a goat get zapped. They just seemed to know. By comparison, bikers in particular were stupid and several showed off at parties by unsheathing their willies and aiming golden streams of pee at a live wire only to jump back in pain.

I have seen goats jump five-foot-high fences from a standing start, and at this, Lobes excelled. She would make an escape not because she had anywhere in particular to go, but just to be ornery. Her usual destination was a smallish Chinese maple I had planted near the house whose shiny red leaves she liked to munch on. If Lobes had been out for a while and hadn't been noticed, and getting noticed was the point of her AWOLs, she would clip clop up onto the kitchen porch and stare in the screen door until she got our attention. If the inside door was closed, she would bleat piteously.

Much of the goat milk was for our own consumption. There was usually a pitcher of chilled milk at mealtimes, for cheese made on a press in the kitchen, and during the Christmas-New Years holiday for eggnog -- or eggnod, as Jack called this potent combination of rum, eggs and goats milk with a pinch of nutmeg.

  The rest of the milk was sold to mothers who were unable to breast feed or were raising lactose intolerant children, some to families who simply wanted to avoid less healthy processed foods, and a fair amount to a woman who had a more modest dairy goat operation on a farm a few miles away. Her place was picture perfect, as opposed to our farm's take-it-or-leave-it atmosphere, which undoubtedly was a turn off to some prospective customers. She couldn't keep up with demand and would buy several gallons a week from us, while never telling her customers the source was our ambiance-impaired farm.

  There was a youngish heiress who had learned of our goats through Davis's girlfriend. She would motor up in a powder blue land yacht of a Bentley Corniche convertible to pick up a gallon or two for her housekeeper's children.   Or so she said.

Milk sales were on an honor system. Visitors parked down the hill outside the milk house, took what they needed from a refrigerator, and left a dollar or two in a cigar box. This the heiress did until she discovered that there was pot to be smoked and beer to be drunk up at the house, so she began parking her Bentley near the kitchen porch and would come inside for a few puffs and a beer or two, pleasures she said her husband forbade her.

One afternoon when the heiress got up to leave, Dadd and I followed her out onto the kitchen porch. There we were greeted by the sight of Lobes standing on the roof of her Bentley, munching on the fabric.

We shouted, Lobes shot us a dirty look and resumed munching. I grabbed her by her spindly back legs and pulled her off the roof and across the trunk. She landed with a thud and gave me a "Well, I never!" look as she adjusted her bustle.

"Don't worry," the heiress said. "I can afford to replace the top."

We were sure she could.

CHAPTER SIX

"Bow-wow-wow-yippie-yo-yippie-yeah
Bow-wow-yippie-yo-yippie-yeah"

Kiln Farm's animals -- and especially the dogs -- were its connective tissue.

Bart was but the first dog in a menagerie that grew to include Spot and Rover, two Lunas, Ruffie, Bugs, Ben and Ged. Even though every breed of dog, and mutts as well, draw from the gene pool of the species *Canis lupus familiaris,* each of ours had distinctive personalities, even in the cases of a mother and daughter and two brothers. If you did not like dogs, you were not welcome, and one housemate short-circuited a budding romance after the woman he was falling for admitted she didn't particularly care for them.

Our dogs, most of them anyway, looked out for us, barking furiously when a car approached, and growling when they sensed a visitor might not have the best intentions. They manipulated us emotionally in ways we would never allow people to do. And we loved it. We loved practically everything they did, from competing to fetch the newspaper in the morning, to resting their heads on our feet when we sat at the kitchen table at night, while there was something sublimely reassuring about looking up while weeding in the garden and seeing them standing guard nearby.

This is not to say we cared more about dogs than people, but we did value their unconditional love and deeply mourned their passing. Besides which, they never cheated, lied or picked fights, didn't get drunk and drive, and as Davis once noted, didn't start wars.

Bart the Irish Setter was the alpha dog, but in name only. He showed no inclination to lead, let alone to do farm dog stuff such as herding and watchdogging. He slept most of the day and would woof at the moon at night. Perhaps he was woofing at deer crossing the pasture below the shed to reach one of the creeks. Or maybe he just woofed for the hell of it.

A big time for Bart was riding in the back of Hawk's pickup truck to the Dairy Queen, where we would buy him a vanilla milkshake and French fries.

Luna arrived at the farm about the same time I did. She was an older German Shepherd with a sweet disposition who was rescued from a man who beat her. We had strong views about abusing animals and believed kidnapping these victims was within our remit, so one night Luna was snatched from the backyard of a house in New Park after we'd heard about the abuse from the girlfriend of her owner.

That owner had a loud voice. Luna would bow her head, tuck her tail between her legs and slink away whenever she encountered men with loud voices at the farm. I am soft spoken and I suppose this is why she took to me. She would pull her arthritic bones up the steps to the attic where she would sleep next to, but never on my bed. That was her choice, not mine. A couple of years on, she had slowed perceptibly and got that look in her eyes dogs have when they know they are not long for this mortal coil. I wasn't surprised when I let out Luna one morning and she went off to die on her own terms. I searched for, but never found her body.

Spot and Rover, brother long-haired Black Labrador crosses belonging to Zarnie, came on the scene not long after Bart and Luna. I would have had trouble telling them apart except that Spot was more of a leader, or I should say instigator, and Rover more of a follower.

This tandem was as energetic as Bart was lethargic, and did everything together. This included being killed seconds apart after crossing the state road, possibly in pursuit of a deer they had spotted while racing through a cornfield ahead of Jack. They were hit about 100 feet apart by the same car.

Jack was well into a trip on four-way orange sunshine LSD; that is, he had done an entire tab instead of a quarter, and was speechless when he saw the carnage. He tried to talk to the very upset elderly couple whose car had hit Spot and Rover but, as he put it, "the smoking crater of my mind was unable to conjure up the right words."

The second Luna was a Golden Retriever belong to Callie and the first of several Dadd bred to males with impeccable pedigrees. There were eight puppies in her first litter and from the time they opened their tiny eyes, one in particular, whom Dadd named Ruffie, stood out because of a serenity about her that belied her tender age. She matured into the most unflappable, Zen-like dog I have ever known. And was a terrific mother.

While the cats took care of rats and mice, woodchucks were another matter. If it hadn't been for the dogs, and primarily Ruffie, these critters would have eaten their way through the garden. She made a sport out of chasing down and killing 'chucks by shaking their necks until they broke. One once took to a tree, and Ruffie sat looking up at her quarry until it got dark and she got hungry.

Dadd bred Ruffie, and one by one most of her pups were sold, usually to families from the New Park suburbs. There were two pups left when a family showed up one day and was escorted to a fenced-in pen above the garden where we had built steps so Ruffie could climb in when she needed to be with her brood.

Everything was going swimmingly. The picture-perfect children were kneeling outside the pen and petting the pups, who licked their hands and faces as they whispered *sotto voce* "Buy me, buy me. I'm only two hundred bucks." The father announced that the only thing to be decided was whether to take one or both pups.

"Both! Both!" the children cried.

Suddenly there was a commotion. Ruffie had appeared on the steps, a bloody 'chuck clenched in her jaws. The mother screamed. The children screamed.

And the father said, "Maybe we'll come back some other time."

Shell finally snared Hawk after years of biding her time. Kind of like Penelope waiting for Ulysses, or so I imagined at the time because I happened to be struggling through Homer's *Odyssey*. They were living together in Colorado and returned to the farm for a visit that coincided with her birthday and a close encounter with a Doberman Pincher nicknamed Bugs whom we were babysitting for a biker friend for a few days. That became a few weeks and finally a few years.

Bugs's ears had never been cropped, hence the Bugs Bunny reference in the name Jack gave him. His original name was Thor or Excalibur or some other power name bikers always seem to give their dogs. This didn't come close to fitting Bugs because he was the least ferocious Doberman I'd ever encountered. He would shiver uncontrollably even in a gentle April shower, could not go outdoors for more than a few minutes in the winter and only then to do his business, and was all sweetness all the time except when around women with shrieky voices.

We -- well, everyone except Dadd -- hatched a plan to throw a surprise birthday party for Shell, although our surprise parties seldom were a surprise. We invited her friends and arranged for one of them to drive her into New Park to shop while we made preparations. This included putting paper lunch bags containing lit votive candles sitting in sand every 20 feet or so along the short driveway.

It was a lovely October evening, the candles were beautiful, and the surprise had somehow held. About 30 people crowded onto the kitchen porch. I turned off the light when I saw Shell's friend's car come up the driveway. Shell got out of the car and I threw on the light.

Shouts of "Surprise! Surprise! Happy Birthday!" rang out.

Shell clapped her hands and declared the moment "Oh so wonderful" in a high-decibel shriek.

No one noticed Bugs working his way through the crowd. He bit Shell hard on the ass and ran.

After he left the farm, Doctor Duck took up with Linnais. She had Aaron, an Old English Sheepdog.

Doctor Duck later brought home to the leather shop a mate for him named Brava.

Linnais was a weaver, so it made a quixotic sort of sense that she wove sweaters and hats from the huge piles of hair she would brush from Aaron and Brava. A comedic result was that dogs, who are consummate sniffers, would be attracted by the smell permeating this clothing, which was especially pungent when wet.

I don't recall how Ben ended up at the farm, but it was likely Pattie had been gifted him. After all, she knew his name. Knowing that Dadd was opposed to more dogs, she made up a story to the effect he had been abandoned.

A cross between a Black Lab and I don't know what else, Ben was immense -- more like a small pony than a big dog. Jack nicknamed him "Football Face" because of his massive forehead and typically blank expression. That expression aside, he quickly sussed out the dynamic of the farm and its critters, people included. From the day he arrived, he was mellow unless a stranger -- to him, at least -- drove up when Pattie's kids were playing in the yard. He then stood at vigilant attention with the ruff on his back bristling like a

Mohawk haircut. Ben would have taken down anyone who tried to get around him, and none dared.

Countenance aside, Ben was terrified of thunderstorms. On one occasion, we arrived home as an especially ferocious storm was abating. We'd left the dogs in the kitchen, but Ben was nowhere to be seen. Then there was a faint scratching noise and some snuffling, which we traced to behind the door under the kitchen sink. There cowered Ben amidst bottles and jars, a pathetic look on his face.

The tulip poplar is the tallest of the Eastern hardwoods with nectar-rich flowers of pale yellow with an orange band that bloom every other spring. Two seedlings popped up in a grassy area between the garden and volleyball court from seeds that had blown in from a host tree which probably was not too far away.

That tree was accidentally found several years later when Luna and Ruffie began disappearing for a half hour or so many days around noon. Dadd and I followed them. It turned out they were slipping away to where a house was being built about a quarter of a mile up the township road. They were mooching handouts from the carpenters during their lunch breaks. Behind the house was a massive tulip poplar, in all likelihood the host tree, perhaps 150 feet high and the tallest of that magnificent species I have ever seen.

"Hey, we don't mind them," one of the carpenters said of our vagabonds. "Actually, we worry when they don't show up."

Ged was a massive white Great Pyrenees whom Pattie named after Ged Sparrowhawk, a heroic character in *Tehanu*, the last book in Ursula K. Le Guin's Earthsea Quartet. Dan gave him to her as a birthday present when he was a puppy.

If Bugs couldn't tolerate the cold, Ged loved it and as befits this magnificent mountain breed, would sleep on the kitchen porch in all but the most bitter weather when he would join the other dogs around the wood stove. A friend describes her first visit to the farm: "There was so much snow that we had to park the Jeep at the foot of a driveway. We had to walk in. The farmhouse eventually appeared, and as we approached the kitchen porch, which was covered in drifting snow, I noticed a big white lump next to the door. The lump was a massive dog, who rose, shook the snow from his coat, and greeted us with an understated woof and enthusiastic tail wags."

Ged loved riding in the back of Dan's station wagon, but had been left behind the night of the accident. If dogs can be emotionally crushed, he certainly was, and looked ceaselessly for Pattie, Caitlin and Jena. He died young and, I believe, of a broken heart.

Rafe, a longtime friend and briefly a housemate, had a dog who was better known than he was. Not necessarily a bad thing when he was on the lam as a member of the Weather Underground, but not necessarily a good thing when he ran for mayor of New Park.

Meatball was probably a mix of Golden and Labrador Retriever and Border Collie. She had brown and white markings not unlike a Guernsey cow, as well as the kind of Zen-like unflappability that Ruffie possessed. If dogs can be cute, she certainly was and then some, and made friends with everyone she and Rafe encountered. When we drove cross country to San Francisco, where Rafe and Meatball had lived for a time, Rafe made a side trip, leaving her in my care. Everywhere I went in the Bay Area, people came up to her and exclaimed, "Oh, it's Meatball!" or words to that effect. Except for a couple of people, none noticed that I wasn't Rafe.

In running for mayor several years later, it was Rafe's intention to shake up a fusty political establishment that had changed little in decades. His campaign got off to a rousing start when Ken Kesey, the novelist of *One Flew Over the Cuckoo's Nest* and Merry Pranksters fame, worked a capacity crowd at a rally at the university theater into a frenzy with a Billy Sunday-esque speech endorsing Rafe. There was just one problem: Candidates for mayor were required to own property and Rafe didn't. This obstacle was ingeniously solved when we passed the hat and bought him a cemetery plot.

Rafe finished behind the incumbent mayor in a three-way race. He was destined to lose, and it probably didn't help that he called his campaign the Meatball Conspiracy.

Bart technically was Doctor Duck's dog, and he took about as good care of him as he did himself.

No one knew Bart's age, but he certainly was up into double digits when he was diagnosed with late-stage cancer that had pretty much eaten up his insides and robbed his magnificent, if usually burr-infested, coat of its deep red luster.

Bart hated to go to the veterinarian so much that he

would pee on himself. Doctor Duck couldn't deal with the situation and there was no way we were going to make Bart draw his last breath on a vet's table. He deserved a better exit, so Hawk and I went out into the field behind the shed and dug a hole. A big hole because Bart was a big guy. I fetched the farm's .22 rifle, but couldn't find the ammunition and had to run into town to buy some. I hoped Bart would die before I returned.

He had not, so I put a single round into the chamber. Having held Bart in my hands so many times over the years while scratching his big knuckle of a head, I knew exactly where to place the muzzle and that I would not need a second shot.

Bart was lying on an overstuffed couch on the front porch that had tumesced into a welter of torn fabric, wood and springs. This was his throne, and two members of his cat harem slept at his side. He barely had the energy to look up as Hawk and I lifted and carried him to the field.

I say with certainty that Bart knew he was going for his last ride, and it wasn't for a shake and fries. When Hawk and I laid him on the carpet of winter wheat and I reached for the rifle, Bart raised his magnificent head one last time. There was the tiniest flicker in those big amber eyes. We knew he was thanking us.

 I am crying as I write this just as Hawk and I cried as we shoveled that dark and incredibly odiferous soil over Bart's body and then got on our hands and knees and patted it down, our tears turning the soil to mud. That was nearly 35 years ago, but I can still smell the soil. And hear Bart woofing at the moon. Perhaps he was woofing at deer crossing the pasture below the shed to reach one of the creeks. Or maybe he just woofed for the hell of it.

CHAPTER SEVEN

*"Bless the daytime / Bless the night
Bless the sun which gives us light
Bless the thunder / Bless the rain
Bless all those who cause us pain."*

Outsiders sometimes called the farm a commune, which it most definitely was not. There was no semblance of a leader, organizational structure or value system -- pardon the term -- as was typical at communes, merely a low-level everyday anarchy.

Doctor Doc and Jane once suggested there be a group meeting. When the appointed date and time arrived, except for the two of them, not a soul was in sight. Meetings were not what the farm was about, besides which it was a Thursday evening and that was when we went out drinking, first at the New Park Tavern, where last call was midnight, and then at the Harding House, a country tavern not far from the farm that served 25-cent draft beers until 2 in the morning.

A cork board on the wall next to the kitchen telephone was ground zero for what group communication there was.

  The board included a shopping list on which we would write our supermarket and natural food co-op wants, a calendar on which reminders of veterinary appointments and other business were scrawled, postcards sent from our travels and those of friends, photographs of those friends' children, prize ribbons from the occasions on which we entered our dairy goats in county fair competitions, and stray pieces of jewelry such as earrings and bracelets that had been abandoned at parties. Nailed to the cork board was a plastic container where bills for rent, people and animal food, electricity, gasoline, and so on went, as well as an accumulation of S&H Green Stamps from supermarket shopping that grew to be about a half-inch thick. The bills were added up at month's end and divided by the number of housemates. While that number rose and fell, my share never exceeded $175 or so. (The Green Stamps eventually were redeemed for a toaster oven, Scotch brand cooler and I forget what else.)

  If the farm were a ship, the kitchen would have been its engine room.

There were three doors in the kitchen -- one to the back porch, one to the rest of the first floor, and one to the back stairway. Three large windows afforded views of the back and side yards and the parking area where the driveways met. The business end of the kitchen included an L-shaped counter with a sink, a hideous pink gas range with a bum pilot light that was a bear to light without singeing your hair, an ancient refrigerator, an early microwave oven that sounded like an Everglades hovercraft, and an inoperable under-the-counter dishwasher. Pots and pans hung from a bar over the stove and there was a narrow aisle behind the counter with barely enough room for a washing machine, big bags of dog and cat food, rice and flour, and a narrow table on which were jars for germinating sprouts and a goat cheese press consisting of a wooden frame and barbell weights.

Ancient knotty pine cabinets hung from the walls on either side of the sink. The far right-hand cabinet sagged badly as a result of a short-lived duck pond that had been dug too close to the house and had compromised the foundation where the kitchen met the old part of the house. There also was a large cupboard next to the refrigerator. I can sometimes be painfully slow on the uptake, and it took *years* before it dawned on me that the cupboard was exactly the size of the first floor windows and it had been built into a window well when the kitchen was added on.

The other end of the kitchen included the telephone, corkboard, wood stove, massive floor-to-ceiling shelves, a large octagonal table and a variety of castoff chairs. These included a rocker that didn't rock and a swivel chair that didn't swivel. A 1950's-era light with a copper hood and two 60-watt bulbs hung over the table. The light had a counterweight that enabled us to lower and raise the hood, atop which were kept a pipe Davis had made in Nam from a mortar shell casing, rolling papers, roach clips and other smoking paraphernalia.

   The kitchen was usually redolent with pleasant smells despite Bigfoot's predilection for passing gas: There was the bubbling potpourri kettle atop the wood stove during cold weather, fresh cut flowers in the late spring and summer, and herbs drying in the late summer and fall.

   Zarnie had crafted the octagonal table from yellow pine, which included beautifully finished parquet-like trim strips on the eight sides, and the legs from framing lumber. He had applied a cherry stain and then several coats of polyurethane. Even after years of heavy use it looked almost new with the exception of bite marks at opposite corners.

Zarnie tired of people oohing and aahing and telling him that his table was "perfect."

"Dammit, nothing is perfect," he exploded as he leaned down at dinner one evening and took a bite out of one of the edges, forever marring its perfectness. Jack was to apply the other bite several years later.

The shelves behind the table were filled with *Organic Gardening* magazines and farming catalogs, canned vegetables, whetstones and lubricating oils for the cutlery and various axes and hatchets, and a large coffee tin that customarily was filled with marijuana. There was an Army-issue flare gun that would be fired to great effect when hunters would jacklight in the fields -- shine bright lights at night in an effort to spot and blind deer, which they would then try to shoot -- while in warm weather there would be a pint Mason jar half filled with isopropyl alcohol into which we deposited the wood ticks the dogs and cats picked up in high grass and the fields. It was gross.

There was a small screwdriver used to tighten the set screw on the knob on the inside of the kitchen door, which regularly came loose. The door had two Plexiglas window panes -- glass panes had kept shattering when we lugged in wood for the stove -- with a crazy quilt array of stickers and decals: Ron-Jon Surf Shops, Audubon Society, American Dairy Goat Association, peace symbol in tie-dye motif, "Boycott California Lettuce" and a "No Jehovahs" warning.

A fair amount of the farm's furnishings and other accoutrements were bought at ridiculously low prices at the auctions that Hawk reconnoitered, sometimes with other housemates in tow. This included the double-wide trailer he found for George I., lawn furniture, a picnic table umbrella with a Cinzano vermouth logo, sickles, scythes and other farm implements, tools, bowls, drinking glasses, flatware, salt and pepper shakers in the shape of toadstools, corn cob skewers that no one ever used, an ice cream churn, and a child's stamped tin Flintstones lunch box filled with darts. This led to the purchase of a dart board which was hung on a disused stereo room door that opened out on the back porch. A photograph of a disgraced Richard Nixon, waving as he boarded Marine Corps One for the last time following his resignation, adorned the center of the dartboard until it had so many holes that it became like so much confetti.

Doctor Doc joked that no one ever moved to the farm for their health, but we ate well. And large.

Sunday dinners were a *tableau vivant* of farm life. There would be as many as a dozen people, including housemates and visitors, crowded around the table, as well as a scrum of slumbering dogs in cold weather, which meant that you had to step carefully when carrying dishes to and from the table. One of us would drive over to fetch George I., who was a frequent guest, as were Wendy and Mik, who would never be confused with the occasional mealtime freeloaders. In summer, mother and son arrived early enough to spend a couple of hours weeding the garden or, in the fall, to help with vegetable freezing and canning.

These dinners included two or three chickens or ducks usually done one of two ways -- on Dadd's grill slathered in his special sauce, or a sort of *coq au vin* baked in the oven by Jane. There were deviled eggs (natch), twice baked potatoes stuffed with goats' cheese or lumpy-by-design mashed potatoes, which were specialties of mine, succotash, pesto on farfalle pasta, Shell's to-die-for banana bread, and stir-fried snow peas with slivered almonds in the spring. In the summer and fall, Vi would toss large salads of several kinds of lettuce, spinach and kale. She garnished them with poke weed, violets and nasturtium, all at hand a few steps from the kitchen porch.

When the harvest of peppers from the garden was at its peak, Dadd would chop four or five varieties and an entire head of garlic, crack several cans of clam sauce and a couple of beers, and cook everything down in a big cast iron skillet. This dish was served on linguini and garnished with cheese grated from a wedge of aged Parmesan that customarily resided on a shelf inside the refrigerator door.

Fast-maturing Silver Queen, a candy-sweet white corn, had recently become available, and we feasted on ear after ear of it in late summer and early fall. There is no culinary experience quite like picking and shucking corn minutes before it goes into a pot of boiling water and then slathering the ears with butter.

There were occasions when we feasted on over-the-top plenty. Returning home from a Pink Floyd concert in Philadelphia one night, we came upon a just-overturned refrigerator truck that had spewed its contents onto the roadway, including cases of filet mignon from Argentina, two of which we purloined. And Eldon, who worked part-time as a longshoreman at a marine terminal near New Park, twice gifted us cases of South Africa rock lobster that had fallen off a refrigerated freighter.

There would usually be a pitcher of chilled goats' milk on the table for dinners and in the summer, lemonade and sometimes homemade ice cream. Preferred ales and beers metamorphosized over the years and betrayed fairly patrician tastes despite our hippy-dippy-ness.

Genesee Cream Ale was supplanted by Rolling Rock, while we had infatuations with Bass Ale and St. Pauli Girl. In later years, there was usually a half keg of Heineken in a refrigerator on the kitchen porch connected to a tap on the fridge door. The annual September release of Löwenbräu Oktoberfest when the centuries-old original was still being imported from Germany was a big deal, but we blacklisted it when Miller bought the venerable brand and turned it into the piss water that passes for many an American brew. There was cognac in cold weather and coffee on demand. After visits to Cuban-influenced Key West, we drank a fair amount of chicory-rich Cafe Bustelo, but our everyday coffee was A&P Colombian, which we ground in an electric coffee mill before brewing to maximize the flavor.

In a rare concession to religion, someone would say grace before we dug in, or, if it was my turn, we would observe a few moments of silence. The table was cleared after dinner, two or three of the guys washed and dried the dishes, and then the ritual passing around of the mortar shell pipe, filled with ice cubes at one end and pot at the other, commenced.

There was a big bucket in the kitchen for food scraps for the chickens and pigs, the first recycling bucket of my acquaintance. Other than Doc, we never preached the organic gospel or any other gospel, nor did we necessarily use organic methods or recycle because of a commitment to save the planet. They just seemed like good ideas.

Doc, possessed with a great intellect and intuitive powers, was well ahead of the rest of us when it came to understanding the planet was running out of the stuff that made it go. He was fond of noting that the U.S. had six percent of the world's population but used 60 percent of its resources. Those numbers seemed to be a little inflated to me, but Doc made an important point, nevertheless, and hammered it home by explaining that the original sin was that man believed he could control nature although he had been on the planet only a short time while nature had devoted millions of years to creating an order to life.

The well under the milk house was naturally artesian and the supply of water seemingly inexhaustible even during the driest summers, but Doc put rainwater barrels around the house and would freak out when people took long showers or left a hose running.

There was nothing new about the New Park Tavern except the video games, and a fresh coat of white paint on the townie and college bar ceilings every year or so after they turned a bilious yellow from cigarette smoke. The tavern's glory days were long in the past and beyond the memories of all but the most elderly tipplers. It underwent a metamorphosis from daytime to nighttime as the old timers moved on and the dirt and decay, as well as the bright glow of the neon beer signs, disappeared behind clouds of cigarette smoke as the placed filled up with college students. The one constant no matter the hour was the smell of cigarettes and beer. The tavern was hot in the summer and cold in the winter, while the men's room floor was on the verge of collapsing into the basement. Which it eventually did.

As the names implied, the townie bar was for locals and college bar for university students. This segregation was not enforced, but we looked down our noses at the mob of university-educated youngsters who stood three and four deep around their bar on most nights. Even though they were only a few years younger than us, we believed ourselves to be worldly wise while they were naifs. We had all the time in the world for anything, or so we thought, while they had no time for anything beyond slamming down beer and doing shots of tequila.

Then there was the jukebox, a beat up old Rock-Ola with a hundred or so 45s, although only a half dozen or so ever seemed to be played -- and played over and over. These included Bob Dylan's "Lay Lady Lay," Arlo Guthrie's cover of "City of New Orleans," Carly Simon's "You're So Vain," the Grateful Dead's "Truckin'," Chicago's "25 or 6 to 4," and a novelty song titled "Loving You Has Made Me Bananas":

> *Oh, your red scarf matches your eyes*
> *You closed your cover before striking*
> *Father had the shipfitter blues*
> *Loving you has made me bananas.*
> *Oh, you burned your fingers that evening*
> *While my back was turned.*
> *I asked the waiter for iodine*
> *But I dined all alone.*

The daytime townie bartender was the diminutive Judy, who wore pink hot pants even in the dead of winter and had mastered the art of mixing cocktails with cigarettes drooping from her lips without the ashes breaking off and dropping into the drinks. Well, most of the time. When an ash did meet a cocktail, she would tell the customer "The drink's on me." Joanie, the nighttime bartender, was a sweetheart once you got beyond her stern countenance. Although she would never let on, she adored us, while new customers and occasionally regulars were greeted with a "Whataya want?" snarl. It was a rare night when Joanie didn't pull a Harmon Killebrew-autographed Louisville Slugger baseball bat from under the bar and scream, "You're outta here!" as she waved it at an offender. There was no bigger insult for Judy and Joanie than being mistakenly called by the other's name.

The rest of the ground floor included a package store, game room and dining room, which was something of misnomer since the menu consisted only of greasy hamburgers and French fries, and even greasier chili cooked up by Dorothy, a black woman who wore an immense platinum blonde wig and would fly into knife-wielding rages if people sent food back. There was a small private dining room for the Thomases, the tavern's owners, who lived in a suite of rooms on the second floor. Actually, Mrs. Thomas was said to be the sole owner because her husband had been convicted of income tax fraud and couldn't hold a liquor license. A large framed black and white photograph circa 1960 hung over a fireplace in their private dining room. The Thomases were standing with a diminutive jockey in a racetrack winner's circle with a thoroughbred that Doctor Duck claimed was the only winner among all the nags they owned and raced prior to buying the tavern.

The package store did a brisk business in six-packs of beer and half-pints of hard liquor. It had a sizable wine selection, including bottles of Chateau Lafite Rothschild and other fine French vintages that were dust-covered remnants from when the tavern served meals on linen tablecloths and chili and burgers were not on the menu. Shoplifting was rampant as Mrs. Pear, who was shaped like one, would doze off behind the cash register after eating the sumptuous-by-comparison dinners that Dorothy prepared for her and the Thomases.

I happened to be present when Jack introduced Doctor Doc to Doctor Duck in the game room, which back in the day included a Foosball table, two pinball machines and Pong and Asteroids, then cutting-edge video games.

"Doctor Doc, this is Doctor Duck."

"Doctor Duck, this is Doctor Doc."

And so it went.

Political correctness would not rear its ugly head for a couple of decades, and the farm was certainly nowhere near politically correct. People were judged for who they were and not for who we might have thought they should be, which was a simple but extraordinarily liberating proposition. We were not a religious bunch, on the whole, although Shell long searched for a path to spiritual enlightenment. Jack had believed in the power of prayer since he escaped with his life from that storm-tossed tugboat, while Doc recoiled at the hypocrisy of well-fed priests sermonizing about the poor when he took his mother to church, although he liked gazing at the light pouring through the stained-glass windows and singing hymns in Latin. I was, and remain, an atheist who reveres in equal measure Jesus, Muhammad, Buddha and John Lennon.

CHAPTER EIGHT

*"I've looked at life from both sides now,
from win and lose, and still somehow
it's life's illusions I recall.
I really don't know life at all."*

There was an imbalance in our little universe. I regret now that the guys didn't give the women more say, and much of the time, we did not treat them as equals. I offer this perspective with some trepidation, because judging the past -- in this case over three decades ago -- by present-day standards can be be a fool's errand.

While some of the women I knew back then insisted on equality and respect, as well as real intimacy in their relationships with men, many did not. Some had not been moved by the gender and sexual revolutions of the late 1960s. Perhaps being their mothers' daughters mattered more, or maybe they were frightened by the great unknown that breaking with traditional roles represented in a still deeply paternalistic society. Where would being liberated take them and what would the emotional price be?

Further complicating the situation was that many men conflated liberation with having sex, and for all I know, still do. But while being sexually liberated for a woman was . . . well, liberating in the sense that it dawned on those who cared about such things in the 1970s that they could have orgasms as often as men, as well as other gender levelers, this did not necessarily carry over to demanding to be liberated in the workplace or society at large. Or at Kiln Farm.

I knew two women during that time who had abortions, one of them because of me.

This woman turned down my offer to take her to a clinic in a big city and pay for the procedure, which left me feeling perhaps I was more liberated than she. In the case of the other woman, the man who had knocked her up wanted nothing to do with her. I ended up driving her to that clinic in the big city -- and sharing the cost of the abortion with the ever generous Eldon -- because she had no money.

Women did most of the farm chores, although it was not beneath the dignity of Dadd or myself to shell peas, and the territorial Pattie did most of the cooking. Jane and Shell took over the kitchen after Pattie's tragic departure. They took turns cooking and fighting over cooking. Jane was a meat eater while Shell was a vegetarian, so their differences were usually over what to put on the table other than poultry, pork and beef. I came to despise lentil loaf and soy burgers, although Shell's vegetarian chili and spinach quiche were quite good.

Jane and Shell alternated packing lunches for Jack and myself when I too took up the nail-bending trade, Jane reliably making something like roast beef or pulled pork sandwiches with horseradish wrapped in homemade bread, and Shell something like goat cheese and sprouts also wrapped in homemade bread, occasionally with a stray hair from her unruly mop.

There were women of my acquaintance who seemed to believe that the only way to survive was to be tough as men. Too bad, because I didn't consider ball busting to be an attribute no matter one's gender. By contrast, the women who lived at the farm provided a soft edge.

Pattie had arrived at the farm with the draft-dodging Denny. She moved in with Dadd after Denny and his alcohol addiction decamped to Oregon. When that relationship grew rough edges, Pattie moved upstairs into the large attic bedroom next to my lair. Dadd took up with Ali, who was a newcomer, and there commenced a series of battles royal between she and Pattie with the kitchen as the arena, although there were also conflicts over milking and egg gathering. Ali hung on for about a year before moving on to a commune in West Virginia.

Later still, Dadd took up with Callie, who was younger than the rest of us and treated with disdain by Pattie *and* Shell. Beyond territorial issues, I suspect both were jealous of her youthful good looks, enthusiastic willingness to help with the chores, and Dadd's affection for her. And that Pattie, being horse crazy, understood that Callie was still more of a filly than a mare, and resented that. She and Shell never succeeded in driving Callie away, and Callie and Shell became fast friends after Pattie's death.

Pattie's and Dan's children had been born in her attic room with the assistance of a midwife. Caitlin and Jena seldom fussed and were a joy even to housemates who had privately grumbled when Pattie twice announced she was pregnant and intended to raise the children at the farm. They were seldom underfoot and little Caitlin was old enough to help with lighter chores by the time of the crash that killed she and her mother.

  Caitlin spent hours on the rope swing and I hours swinging her as she giggled and cried, "higher, higher!," her ringlets of platinum blonde hair bouncing to and fro. Our other simple pleasure was doing an exaggerated dance sort of like that of the ancient Egyptians pictured on temple walls. (Shell called this *sneathing*, a made-up word, or so she thought, until a couple of years later when we were in San Francisco and I drove her out to the home of an old girlfriend in the suburb of Pacifica. The girlfriend lived on Sneath Lane.)

  Caitlin and Jena loved to be read to. Jena was too young to understand, but I suspect paid attention because her big sister did. Berenstain Bears books were oft requested, as was *'Twas the Night Before Christmas* no matter the time of year. But Caitlin's favorite was one of my own books as a child, the title now forgotten, about Tommy, a brave lad who endured being teased because he played the tuba. He becomes a hero when he warns of a shipwreck by tooting on his maligned instrument, with the accompanying words

> *Many brave hearts are asleep in the deep,*
> *So beware! Beware!*

which I would intone in a tuba-like voice, going lower and lower until I inevitably cracked up Caitlin and her sister.

The deaths of Caitlin and her mother, and subsequent departure of Jena, who was raised by friends of father Dan's family, left an enormous hole that never was filled. Caitlin had a set of wooden building blocks with a letter on one side and a number on another that she would play with on the floor of the Phone Booth. With a heavy heart, I eventually packed up the blocks and her other toys, but did not notice until a few days later that the "Y" block had become wedged in a corner. I have placed this block where I can see it everywhere I have lived since leaving the farm. "Y" as in "Why did this have to happen?" I am no closer to finding the answer than after the crash.

One of the biggest lies told about the farm was that we were sybarites and our lives were a nonstop orgy.

As a result of this codswallop, some women who came to our parties apparently feared that when the evening grew late they would be thrown over menfolk's shoulders and taken upstairs and molested. Or something. So they would leave early. I learned this later, or sussed out as much, when I would be introduced to a woman by someone who would note that I lived at the farm, and her reaction would be to turn ashen and then turn heel lest I fondle her backside. Or something.

For the prurient-minded, the reality would have been a letdown.

While one woman housemate slept with several of the guys before settling down, so did millions of other women in the 1970s. I myself slept with a number of women, only one of them a housemate. There were always women at our parties who would be delighted to be taken upstairs, some of whom we obliged. In my case, this included twin sisters over successive nights of partying.

The only overt sexual display I ever saw at the farm was a scene out of a bad stag film: A very drunk and totally naked Suzy Creamcheese, as Jack called her, climbed onto the kitchen table in the midst of a Flag Day party and frigged herself.

🏠

Like Doctor Doc, Pattie understood the frailty of the environment although she didn't have the academic underpinnings that informed his activism. Nothing made her angrier than when people would leave us their trash. The cats and dogs abandoned at the ends of the driveways were one thing, but bags of sodden trash were quite another.

Pattie struck back after she got Big Blue, a Chevy Impala sedan. She sifted through an especially fetid gift, and among the milk cartons, egg shells and newspapers, found an envelope with an address in a pricey housing development near New Park. The trash went into Big Blue's cavernous trunk and off went Pattie to the housing development, where she dumped the trash in the backyard sandbox of the culprits' children.

Pattie told me before she died, and Shell years later, that they bristled at what they saw as the farm's unstated *status quo* -- that women were expected to stay in their place, although neither of them ever made an issue of it.

This was sadly ironic because both strived to be independent, although growing up, neither woman was encouraged to succeed as their older brothers were. Most important to their antediluvian mothers was that they make good impressions when they met people. Shell had a more conventional rite of passage. She went to college and then was briefly and unhappily married to her high school sweetheart. Pattie had been in and out of a mental institution as a teenager. It was not because she was crazy. It was because of a father and mother who were crazy in their unrelenting opposition to her adolescent rebelliousness and expectation that she aspire to nothing more than finding a nice man to father children. When she opened up to me about her stays in the "nut hut," as she called it -- revealing that she hadn't been able to talk about that awful period of her life with anyone else except for a single girlfriend -- she described it as time standing still.

  Pattie and Shell had something else in common: A little-girl fascination with fairies. Yes, like Tinkerbell, and specifically the so-called Cottingley Fairies, a series of photographs of fairies taken by two young girls in the garden of their English home in 1920. Spiritualists had promoted the photos as proof of the existence of supernatural creatures, and despite criticism by skeptics, no less a personage as Sir Arthur Conan Doyle, author of the Sherlock Holmes mysteries, endorsed the accuracy of the images. It was in the late 1970s, not long after Pattie was killed, that the photos were definitively debunked.

Two woman housemates believed there never was an imbalance.

Teana recalls her on-and-off residency at the farm as the happiest time of her life, and aside from Dadd's occasional grouching about the manner in which she and Vi weeded the garden, a complaint that did not seem to extend to the men, she soaked up the farm's self-sustaining nature. The experience sparked a life-long love of gardening, and she spent many years as a private gardener.

Vi said she went from being an abused woman to a princess when she moved into the small bedroom across the hallway from my lair through which we could go up onto the roof. She called it The Room With The Hatch To The Universe.

"I realized that I didn't have to wear makeup and panty hose," she once told me. "It was tremendously liberating."

Pattie was in the habit of leaving notes on my dresser, some asking if I could do the milking for her because she would be away and others expressing appreciation for our friendship. A note she had written to me was found in a back pocket of her jeans after the crash.

One note I hold especially dear was written inside a birthday card with a maiden surrounded by a menagerie of animals, including the obligatory unicorn:

> *May your day be overflowing*
> *with sunshine and giggles.*
> *Don't ever let the romantic in you slip away.*
> *May magic live within you*
> *and may it surround you forever.*

Pattie was big on premonitions, and fortunately the bad premonitions except for one about the crash, never came to pass. This premonition led her to show me where the things she most valued were kept, including a stained glass jewelry case filled with trinkets, notes and letters, and a journal with deckle-edged pages covered with paisley print cloth that was about half filled with musings, many of them reflecting her streak of romanticism, written in a schoolgirl scrawl. All were secreted in a nook in the wall behind the headboard of her bed. She wanted me to have these things should anything happened to her, and do with them what I thought was best.

What I wanted to do was pass on this stuff to Jena when she was old enough to perhaps understand what the mother she hardly knew was all about, but I never did. Jena must be in her early 30s now.

CHAPTER NINE

*"Everyone will start to cheer
when you put on your sailin' shoes"*

It soon became obvious that the privacy Doctor Duck and Davis had sought in moving to Kiln Farm was slipping away one weekend at a time.

Every Saturday and some Sundays became a party as word got around in New Park that a good time was to be had at a hippie farm not far out of town. It was not unusual to have 10 or 15 people, most of them freeloaders, show up uninvited.

Because we were not inclined to hold meetings, decisions were made through a sort of group osmosis. The Gordian Knot of the uninvited visitor problem was cut with the birth of the first Flag Day party, so named because it was held on a June 14, which happened to be Flag Day, a once celebrated, but now overlooked national holiday except for sales at shopping malls.

Out of this decision evolved a simple rule: If you didn't have an invite, you weren't welcome at the farm. Except on Flag Day.

The first party was memorable for its sheer zaniness. We had run into some Rainbow Tribe adherents in the Florida Keys the previous winter. This loosely affiliated group holds annual events known as Rainbow Gatherings, which are excuses to get high with a few thousand close friends. Anyhow, we invited these folks to stop by the farm. Which they did en route to their annual gathering in Vermont with an uncanny sense of timing, arriving in their jalopy of a converted school bus on the very morning of the first party.

Someone on the bus had a box of faux pearl clip-on neckties, and before long most everyone, including the dogs and goats, were wearing neckties. Zarnie had mailed me peyote buttons, so some of us were tripping.

From the beginning, the parties attracted bikers and their women, who made deafening entrances and exits on their chromed Harley Davidsons with booming revs and gear changes. There was never a helmet in sight.

While some bikers can be unpleasant, most who came to our parties were pussycats once the leather-and-chains bullshit was stripped away. A friend remarked that our parties were so much fun because, as she put it, "People didn't impose their personal shit." That included bikers, who could be aggressive in other settings like the townie bar at the New Park Tavern, but toned down their group act in our presence, confining their macho banter to mocking people who wore sissy helmets and rode Japanese motorcycles or, worst of all in their view, BMW two-wheelers.

The parties were great levelers. There would be a biker talking to a college professor, a longhair hoisting shots of tequila with a volunteer fireman, a Civil War re-enactor chatting up a biker chick, and a grandfather dancing with a young lass. With one exception, there never was a fight, and with one other exception, we never had to threaten to kick anyone off the farm.

The fight, between two hothead musicians over whose turn it was to play, occurred a few hours into the inaugural Flag Day Party. One of them was the man who had abused Luna.

The girlfriend of Luna's former tormenter, a petite and fiery redhead, broke up the fight and then climbed up the chest of her boyfriend until she was eye to eye with him. *Bam! Pop!* Her first punch bloodied his nose and broke his glasses; the second knocked out a tooth. The girlfriend scrammed, and I took the boyfriend upstairs to the bathroom to clean him up. The tough guy demeanor had evaporated and between sobs he kept saying, "I'll never be able to play the flute again! I'll never be able to play the flute again!"

He never noticed Luna, or if he did, he didn't care that his disappeared dog had somehow reappeared at the farm.

One partygoer had a proclivity for getting smashed and screaming *yahooo!*, *aaagh!* and other banalities at the top of his lungs. We named him The Screamer. At one party, he became so annoying -- as well as a magnet for complaints to the state police by neighbors -- that we threatened to tie him up inside the bucket of Doctor Duck's surplus Army Corps of Engineers bucket truck and elevate the arm to its 35-foot height. He quieted down fast.

The Screamer had lost two fingers on one hand after messing around with fireworks. He had scars from bad burns on a forearm, only one eye as the result of some calamity or another, and was minus a lower leg after the second Flag Day party, which was additionally memorable because he had commandeered the stereo and played Queen's "Bohemian Rhapsody" over and over at deafening volume.

  The amputation was a consequence of his passion for driving his 1952 Plymouth coupé flat out. The car was T-boned at an intersection near New Park by a pickup truck driven by an innocent who didn't see the black blur traveling at 100 miles an hour. The pickup driver was okay, but an ambulance crew was only able pull The Screamer from what was left of the Plymouth after cutting off his left leg at the knee. The rest of the leg and foot had been crushed in a tangle of sheet metal. The Screamer proudly refused to be fitted with a prosthetic limb and got on with an aluminum crutch. This was a handy pointer, and a poker if he felt he was being crowded.

  The Screamer was a gifted restorer of cars and motorcycles. How unfortunate it wasn't something less perilous such as fixing up Radio Flyer wagons. After coming home from the hospital, he worked for months restoring an early Jaguar E-Type convertible that he and his father had found mouldering in a garage. He did a superb redo down to the chrome-plated hood latches and a one-off hand clutch on the steering column since he couldn't reach the clutch with his partially amputated leg. He painted the Jag a gorgeous cobalt blue, I suspect to match his eye patch.

The farm was the destination on the restored Jag's maiden run. The Screamer proudly showed off his masterwork and offered to take us for rides. We were not crazy, at least not that crazy, and he found no takers. The day wore on and The Screamer got pretty sloshed. We tried to sober him up, but eventually he roared off into the sunset with a fair amount of alcohol on board. A few minutes later, the Jag was totaled at the same intersection. This time, The Screamer walked away from the crash -- or I should say, hobbled away -- with just a few cuts. The Jag, however, was totalled.

As the third Flag Day party approached, our friend Phyllis suggested that the price of admission should be a flag.

A few people complied and there were perhaps 10 flags that year, another 10 the following year, and eventually 40 or so we hung on fences and clotheslines rigged between trees. This colorful assemblage included several American flags, including one with the original 13 stars and another with 48, a couple of skull-and-crossbones pirate flags, several state flags, two flags that had flown over firebases in Nam, a Conch Republic flag, tie-dyed flags, a Jimi Hendrix flying eyeball flag, and some hand-sewn flags, including one with the bold letters *BEST EVER!*, a pet phrase of Jack's embroidered by Jane onto a crazy quilt-like field.

Some of the flags would go home with their owners at the end of a party, while the rest were stored in a steamer trunk secreted behind a table in the living room.

By the fourth Flag Day party, people were showing up on Friday evening, there were hundreds on Saturday, and only a few less on Sunday. Cars were parked along the long driveway all the way down to the state road. There were eventually 500 or 600 partygoers over the course of a weekend. Waves of people surged around the house and poured in and out of it. These occasions were just about the only times that the door to the center staircase and the fun house of the second floor hallway was opened. This blew many a mind.

The parties evolved into scenes. Or rings, I suppose, because they certainly were circuses. A walk around and into the house revealed:

The beer scene off the kitchen porch, mostly guys who guarded the kegs, kept them iced and tapped new kegs when old ones blew. This area inevitably devolved into a sea of beer-saturated mud.

The black walnut tree scene involved folks who would loll in the grass around little Caitlin's rope swing and take turns swinging their kids or themselves.

The bluegrass scene with a circle of musicians playing acoustic guitars, banjos and sometimes autoharp and harmonica. We were twice honored by the presence of Ola Belle Campbell Reed, the great folk songwriter, singer and banjo player, who along with her son and assorted other members of a pick-up band, played far into the night.

The garden scene above my bicycle wheel weather vane with folks contemplating the veggies and flowers, and sometimes their navels.

The volleyball scene that was Jungle Rules, only. This meant randomly chosen sides, an utter absence of strategy and even less ball control.

The front porch scene was the gallery for the horseshoe match scene.

The kitchen scene was reminiscent of an Old Masters painting -- although it took a certain state of mind to see it that way -- with a dozen or so people crowded around the big octagonal table. They smoked huge quantities of marijuana from the mortar shell pipe. The smoke would become so thick that the ceiling disappeared. A vacated seat was quickly snapped up by an on-call stoner.

The stereo room scene was a mass of writhing, sweaty dancers packed impossibly close together as music -- a variety of artists and bands early in the evening, but always cassette tapes of Grateful Dead concerts as the night grew old -- pounded out from Davis's speakers. The floor heaved up and down from the gyrations of the dancers. I was amazed it never gave out.

On the few Flag Day weekends when it happened to rain, and our typically good luck extended to the meteorological aspects of party weekends, the sea of mud extended from the kegs onto the kitchen porch, into the kitchen, and up the back stairs to the second floor hallway and bathroom.

The bathroom was overtaxed under normal circumstances, yet we couldn't very well keep partygoers from using it. A solution of a sort, which sort of worked, was to tape a sign on the door that read:

> *If all you have to do is pee,*
> *please take yourself to the outhouse*
> *in the upper garden. Thank you.*

Early on the parties were pretty much all beer all the time. I counted 14 half kegs at the outset of one party (which translate into about 2,300 12-ounce beers) before the hat was passed later in the day and volunteers were dispatched to buy additional kegs. One biker, who distinguished himself by riding his Harley full out with a lit cigar in his mouth, would throw in a hundred dollar bill each year.

  Then a nice thing happened: People, acknowledging our hospitality and perseverance, if not often coming right out and saying so, showed up with more and more food, some of which they cooked on Dadd's barbeque grill, which had been fabricated by a welder friend from half of a 55-gallon oil drum cut lengthwise and hinged to the other half so it could be raised and lowered. Genielle made a pâté from duck livers. At later parties there was also a pig that was slaughtered on the eve of a party, stuffed with sauerkraut, sauteed and turned on a spit in a fire pit for 10 or so hours until the meat practically fell off the bones.

  The pig had an unintended effect. Dogs were not welcome at parties, although early on people brought them anyway. This meant there were sometimes dog fights, including a memorable scrap between a wee black Scottie and an immense Husky. The fight only ended when the dogs were pulled apart by their tails. Our own dogs never fought, but could be a pain when there were so many people to beg food from. They would gorge themselves on pig scraps, then wander away to sleep off their Other White Meat hangovers.

  Then a really nice thing happened: Ricardo, who became the executive chef at the New Park Tavern after the elderly owners retired, supplemented Dadd's too-small grill with a professional gas grill the size of a small car. He would cook hamburgers, hot dogs, sausage and bratwurst for all comers, the meat, buns and condiments supplied gratis by the tavern, with an assist from Double Doug, a corpulent sous chef and Santa Claus lookalike so nicknamed to distinguish him from Single Doug, a more economically sized Doug who worked in the tavern kitchen. Whether their bosses were aware of their largesse was not known.

  Then another really nice thing happened: Bryce, an alcoholic who typically left parties a drunken mess, sobered up. He and his wife would show up on Sunday mornings, their van filled with eggs, sausage, bacon, toast, butter and condiments, and cook breakfast for everyone on the gas grill. It was, a mutual friend said years later, Bryce's way of atoning and thanking us for indulging him.

If you measured the success of Flag Day parties by the number of state police cars that responded in later years to neighbors' noise complaints, the final party was a four-car spectacular with a touch of comic relief when one police cruiser bottomed out in an especially deep rut in the long driveway and had to be towed away.

We had banned electric bands from the last several parties. We encouraged people to bring tents and sleeping bags rather than drive home, which they did in ever greater numbers, transforming the lawn above the garden into a Kampground of America with tie-dyed accents.

But the parties still got out of hand. The children of partygoers who had been toddlers in earlier years were now teenagers, and more likely than not to emulate their parents, kids from the suburbs were crashing the scene, and too many underage visitors were drinking beer and smoking dope. The bills for long-distance calls made from the kitchen phone during parties had become ridiculously high. Somebody was going to get hurt. The barn was going to get burned down. Something really bad was going to happen. Worse than someone merely losing part of a leg in a car crash.

After another of those group osmosis decision-making moments, it was agreed the following Flag Day weekend we would put sawhorses at the driveway entrances with signs hanging from them that read:

No Flag Day Party
No Kidding

People came anyway, some of them because Doctor Duck whispered to acquaintances at the tavern that while the official line was the previous year's party had been the finale, this was just a ruse to keep the riff raff out. This was kind of rich, because we could certainly be considered riff raff ourselves.

We loved Doctor Duck like a brother -- as he said, we're all brothers and sisters on the face of the planet Earth -- but we could have killed him, and it would have been a case of justifiable homicide. As it was, he accomplished that on his own, drawing his last breath two days before a gorgeous non-Flag Day party weekend several years later. It was his turn to be the guest of honor at a "going-away party" at the funeral home next to his leather shop.

CHAPTER TEN

*"We're jammin', jammin',
and I hope you like jammin', too"*

  This is the story of how, among other things having to do with music, the late great Bob Marley ended up at Kiln Farm.

  In 1966, three years before the farm began to come back from the dead, Marley married Rita Anderson. Frustrated over a stalled music career in Jamaica, he and his bride moved into his mother's house in a neighborhood of Jamaican ex-pats in a city near New Park. He worked briefly at a chemical company laboratory and then on the assembly line at an auto manufacturing plant in New Park, an experience that inspired him to write the song "Night Shift," before returning to Kingston. The rest, as they say, was history as Marley went on to become the first reggae superstar.

  I was an early convert to reggae. My introduction came during the summer of 1973 when I was on a road trip and the soundtrack from the film *The Harder They Come*, by reggae trailblazer Jimmy Cliff, was played through the house system between the sets of a Jerry Garcia Band show in Berkeley, California.

Reggae was something else. I was knocked over by the swinging backbeat, Cliff's mellifluous vocal stylings, and always have been a sucker for the minor chords that suffuse reggae, which can induce a kind of hypnotic effect on me. (Some violin and accordion music does the same thing.) The next day, I bought my first two of what became dozens of reggae albums – *The Harder They Come* soundtrack and, on the recommendation of a record store clerk, *Catch a Fire*, Marley's debut American album .

Meanwhile, back at the farm we had found a solution to a nagging problem: Male kid goats are a drag on a dairy operation but goat meat is enjoyed by certain ethnic groups who serve it on holidays, for weddings and other special occasions, while it is a staple of the Jamaican diet. So we put a classified ad offering male kids for sale in a newspaper published in the city where Marley's mother lived. We ended up selling kids to several Greeks and Italians for Easter feasts, and the first of many to Marley's uncle, Malcolm.

Thus began a mutually respectful relationship with the reggae star's extended family. While the farm would not be confused with Nine Mile, the hamlet in rural St. Ann Parish where Marley was born, when his relatives visited us in warmer weather they weeded our garden with abandon. They were welcome to pick as much produce as they wanted and as much pig weed as they could stuff into garbage bags. We eventually just gave kid goats to Malcolm, who would take them out behind the silos and out of sight of the other goats, slit their throats and skin them in one deft swoop.

While we had long ago beaten back the jungle that preceded the garden, pig weed would come up each spring like clockwork because we did not use the chemicals that would lay low the weed. The prickly leaves of this hardy member of the amaranth family are a Jamaican delicacy, edible after several *hours* of steaming. Malcolm and his posse prepared it as a side dish to goat's head soup.

Yes, goat's head soup.

This concoction is what the name implies. Considering the smell emanating from the bubbling stew pot on our stove, a reasonable facsimile of which is on offer on the cover of The Rolling Stones' *Goat's Head Soup* album, it took great willpower to eat even a few spoonfuls, which we did out of politeness when Malcolm would roll up his sleeves and take over Sunday dinner.

Throw a crew like ours together and there are likely to be different musical tastes.

Hawk, Dadd and Doctor Doc tended toward bluegrass and Texas swing like the Nitty Gritty Dirt Band, Bill Monroe, David Grisman and Asleep at the Wheel. Bix liked anything with bass guitar, which he played. Pattie's tastes tended more toward the romantic (Joni Mitchell and Jackson Browne) and the romantically melancholy (Tim Buckley). Jack liked anything with a beat and for a while was obsessed with Bachman Turner Overdrive, a phase that mercifully passed. Davis's tastes tended toward the psychedelic, while Doctor Duck was passably good at playing the fiddle, but didn't really seem to be into music. I can't remember him ever putting anything on the stereo room turntable.

My tastes were eclectic and on offer in the six cassette tapes that I took to Nam -- The Beatle's *Abbey Road*, Judy Collins' *Wildflowers,* Bob Dylan's *Nashville Skyline*, Stan Getz's *Getz/Gilberto*, Bach's *Brandenburg Concerto*, and the Rolling Stones' *Let It Bleed*, which was especially appropriate given the surroundings.

Like many high school kids of my generation, I fell hard for soul, rhythm and blues and, of course, the British Invasion bands. I had been introduced to jazz by way of the Dave Brubeck Quartet at the tender age of 14. College brought the cross fertilization of folk (Ian and Sylvia, Joan Baez, Gordon Lightfoot) and rock (Crosby, Stills, Nash and Young in all their incarnations). With my introduction to psychedelics, I fell hard for the usual suspects (Jimi Hendrix and Pink Floyd, chief among them). Then there was reggae.

But my main men were the Grateful Dead, who I saw in concert for the first time in the fall of 1967 following the Summer of Love and many more times over the years.

I was initially attracted by the Dead's acid suffused jamming and wordplay. Lyrics like

> *Dark star crashes*
> *Pouring its light into ashes*
> *Reason tatters*
> *The forces tear loose from the axis*

from "Dark Star," a modal vamp that could run to 20 minutes or longer and had a profound effect on my youngish sponge of a mind even if I did conclude later that the words were pretty much off-the-cuff nonsense. Then there was the Dead's bluegrass side and their wonderful catalog of Americana songs (think "New

Speedway Boogie," "Jack Straw" and, of course, "Truckin") that grew out of Jerry Garcia's collaboration with Robert Hunter, who is as good a songwriter as the gods of Tin Pan Alley. Then there was "Brokedown Palace," which was to become an anthemic metaphor for the farm when it no longer was, and the lyrics to which are the coda to this book.

   Life can be messy and so were the Dead. Unlike many stars, Garcia did not seek out fame. At heart an unassuming man who just wanted to play music, fame found him. And despite a long career as an extraordinary composer and guitarist that brought him adulation, gold records and eventually wealth, happiness remained elusive. He was never able to get the addictive drug monkey off his back for very long once it climbed on. Technically, heroin finally killed him, or rather his heart, but I believe that fame was the real culprit.

   But for a while, and that very much included the 1970s, things were good. The Dead's sound was so technically sophisticated, with an unheard of clarity and purity, that it took other bands years to catch up sonically. The Dead's concerts were so popular that their front office set up a system through which their most devoted fans had first dibs at tickets, the band would only play in cities where arena managers and the police would permit camping, and they tithed a considerable amount of their profits to charities.

Not unlike the farm, the Dead's success was accidental and at the same time preordained because of the times. Garcia liked to call their popularity a "miraculous manifestation." I call it synchronicity. Then there was my favorite bumper sticker of the era:

> *Who are the Grateful Dead, and why do they keep following me?*

My Dead-centricism (Terrapin the cat wasn't so named for nothing) was the cause of the few times there were disagreements over what was played on the stereo.

Davis's speakers were complimented by a pair of JBL studio monitors I hung from ceiling hooks in the corners of the kitchen behind the octagonal table. Depending upon who was doing what and where, the speakers in the stereo room and kitchen could be played or bypassed, which meant that if the folks in the kitchen didn't want to hear what was being played, those who did could gravitate to the stereo room.

Absent a television and the dearth of decent FM stations, there was music most evenings and on afternoons and evenings on most weekends, but the Dead's spacier stuff had to be saved for later hours because Doc and Dadd weren't into music that, for wanted of a better description, wasn't literal. Dadd would become grouchy and go up to his room, while Doc would declare in Latin that this jam or another wasn't music, it was *strideo stridere stridi*, which roughly translated as a harsh noise.

   Then there were Sunday mornings when I would put on an LP of Ravi Shankar ragas or Bach's *Goldberg Variations* before anyone else was up save for Pattie, who would be down milking the goats.

   The Allman Brothers Band was a fave, and I was fortunate enough to see them twice shortly before Duane Allman, the band's leader and a slide guitar player without peer, died in a motorcycle crash.

   The band's *Live at Fillmore East* album is perhaps the best non-Grateful Dead live album ever, and "In Memory of Elizabeth Reed" is the album's masterpiece.

   As guitarist Dicky Betts slowly tricks out the song's primary theme, he is joined by the creamy signature slide sound of Allman's guitar. They gallop into a quasi-Latin beat, trade solos, then a series of ever more furious peaks that beg comparison to a John Coltrane saxophone solo, and finally a thunderous climax.

It wasn't until a few years into the decade that someone pointed out there is a tombstone in a New Park cemetery along the railroad track where Edward was killed on which is inscribed "In Memory of Elizabeth Reed." I had to see for myself. They were right.

Early on, the farm was a haven for bands from New Park, which had a vibrant music scene but not enough places to perform beyond a few coffee houses, a club called the Lead Balloon, the back room of the New Park Tavern, as well as the garages and basements of folks in the New Park suburbs who didn't care if their neighbors' minds were blown. Among the bands were Big Dog Road, Martha Lidd, Primeval Slime, Jack of Diamonds, Rudy Baker and the Vegetables, Canyon, Scuzzy Frogg, Rockett 88, Bad Sneakers and George's Lunch ("Take us out or eat us here"). Then there was Snakegrinder and the Shredded Fieldmice, the farm's house band.

Weird things happened to and around Snakegrinder.

Their manager was seriously injured in a skydiving accident, while longtime friend and brief housemate Rafe was visited by the ghost of lead signer Edward a few days after he was run over by that train. Edward informed Rafe that he would take his place in the band within a year although Rafe had never sung in performance. Sure enough, about a year later, two band members asked him to join Snakegrinder, which he did after a cross-country trip with me during which he honed his vocal chops and graduated from playing the kazoo to the harmonica, which he mastered after many hours of leaning out of my bus window to practice so as to not disturb Meatball and myself. A little further on, Big Dog Road opened for Snakegrinder at a house party. Among their songs was one about a shopping mall that included the lyric

*We don't have the balls to walk through the walls,
but at least we have the brains to stay out of the way of trains*

As "trains" came out of the lead singer's mouth all of the band's amplifiers blew. The ghost of Edward was angry.

The members of Snakegrinder were great if sometimes aloof musicians, but they had problems: Difficulty getting gigs because club owners knew that their fans were more interested in toking up in the parking lot between sets than buying beers, which begat a financial crisis that ended only when the band broke up, while no one was able to categorize their music. Not that it mattered. Best I could figure, Snakegrinder was influenced by the psychedelic movement with dollops of South-Southwest and anarchic folk-rock flavors. They also did original songs, most of them on the idiosyncratic side. These included a lengthy opus titled "Nothing's Very Easy When Your Baby's in the Lake" that included a lyric that was to become the title of this book.

Some New Park bands were quite good, others not nearly as good as their names were clever, and two were upstaged by a precocious teenager, who was rebuffed when he asked to sit in, at that Halloween party my first night at the farm.

Canyon, a band made up of Nam veterans, was first up and acquitted themselves well. Then came Snakegrinder, which jammed past the midnight hour. Last up was the teenager who tore down the house as he raced from blues standard to blues standard, including "Move It On Over" and "Madison Blues."

His name was George Thorogood, just out of high school and headed for stardom because he was so good at connecting with audiences. So good that when he and his Destroyers opened for the Rolling Stones a few years later in the first show of the lamely named "American Tour 1981," they electrified the hordes at

100,000-seat JFK Stadium in Philadelphia. Journey, the supposedly hot second act, did a limp set and eventually left the tour because George and the Destroyers upstaged them at that and every other show. Meanwhile, "Move It On Over" and "Madison Blues" became huge hits.

Several roommates, usually Jack and Shell, went on road trips with me to see the Dead notable for the miracle of our arriving back at the farm in one piece. I liked to think of my bus as like a cowboy's loyal horse who always knows the way home. The worst thing that happened over the years I followed the Dead was accidentally washing a baggie of pot I had left in a back pocket of dirty jeans after coming in off the road. This I did several times.

On one expedition, we caught four shows in upstate New York on consecutive nights, the first in Rochester, when we walked into the hall just as the band broke into "Eyes of the World," a favorite, and the last at Cornell University in Ithaca, which many Deadheads of my vintage consider to be the band's best show ever.

In typical Dead style, they took us to amazing places during a four-hour extravaganza in Barton Hall,

Cornell's packed and acoustically sublime Gothic Revival performance space, elevating us to great and then greater heights, and then bringing us down ever so gently at the end. Although it was May, snow was falling when we walked out of the hall. The perfect touch to end a perfect evening.

The shows in between were in Syracuse and Binghamton. Shell nearly missed the Binghamton show. We were idling outside the arena when a guy offered her a toke on a joint. I quickly recognized that it had been dosed with angel dust, better known as PCP, a harsh and deadly powerful hallucinogenic with a telltale stench. Shell had already begun to inhale when I snatched the joint from her. She quietly passed out in my arms, but shortly came to.

Later that year we saw the band at the Capitol Theater in North Jersey. We felt confined in our seats and retired to the back of the hall. Jack is a man of many allergies, or at least was then. Anything smelling of roses would send him into paroxysms of sneezing.

A woman strolled behind us reeking of rose perfume. Jack commenced his first *achoo!* just as the Dead broke into one of their standards, "It Must Have Been the Roses."

Shell was cheerfully tone deaf and had a knack for mangling Dead lyrics. For instance, the lyric

Like street cats making love

from the song "Looks Like Rain" became

Like streetcars making love

When Jack pointed out that it was street cats and not streetcars, Shell bemusedly responded, "but the Dead are from San Francisco. Streetcars, ya know."

Among the other Jamaican visitors to Kiln Farm were Marley's wife Rita and several of their kids, including Ziggie, then not long out of diapers and destined to become heir to his father's throne. But The Man himself never appeared until a day -- and it was the rarest of days -- when no one was home.

Pattie did the evening milking. She opened the cigar box where people would leave money for milk. There was a $20 bill folded into a scrap of paper on which was scrawled:

Thanks for the milk. Love Ya! Bob Marley

CHAPTER ELEVEN

*"I hear you knocking, But you can't come in
I hear you knocking, Go back where you've been"*

One of the less enchanting aspects of life at Kiln Farm was the knowledge that someone uninvited and unwelcome could show up at any time. These interlopers meant well, for the most part, but were usually darkening our door because they had nowhere else to go. The farm's number was in the phone book, but under the name of Sam Green, a photographer who had built the Phone Booth during a brief sojourn with Doctor Duck and Davis. When wannabes who were not necessarily in our good graces would ask for the number preparatory to darkening that door, Jack would deadpan that it was Tidewater 10-09, the number immortalized in "New Jet to the Promised Land," the great Chuck Berry song.

Rafe, he of Meatball the dog fame, didn't merely dodge the draft like Denny, he actively opposed it. As well as the war and everything to do with the U.S. government.

He was a member of Students for a Democratic Society before dropping out of the university in New Park. He joined the ultra-radical Weather Underground after being beaten by the Chicago police and jailed, without cause, during the 1968 Democratic National Convention.

As someone who thought about fleeing to Canada to avoid the draft and a ticket to Nam for about . . . uh, five seconds, I admired Rafe for his determination to swim against a tide that I and many other members of our generation let carry us, some to our deaths. He had been on an FBI fugitive list for a couple of years when he tracked me down at the farm and pleaded with me to allow him to hide out there for "a while." He had a paranoid side, which I suppose he had earned, and was convinced that a squad of G-men was a step or two behind him, which was unlikely because by his own admission he was a small cog in the big Weather Underground wheel.

"How long is a while?" I asked.

No answer.

A beloved aunt who lived with Rafe's mother in New Park was gravely ill. Rafe assumed that their house was under surveillance, so he couldn't exactly present himself at the front door. However, his brother, Eldon, lived at home and always parked in the garage, so he was able to sneak inside by hiding in the back of Eldon's van.

"Okay," I said. "Just don't tell anyone you're a fugitive."

He nodded.

Rafe had taken up house painting while on the lam and would paint over those hideous bathroom walls in a soothing eggshell white in return for being able to have a place to crash. He got more paint on the fixtures and himself than the walls and should probably have stuck to the revolution.

McFire was a former circus roustabout who drove up one day in what had to be one of the first conversion vans, the back of which was emblazoned with bumper stickers like:

If You See This Van A Rockin'
Don't Come A Knockin'

Out of work and down to his last few food stamps, or so he said, McFire needed a place to stay. There was no room in the house, so he slept in his van most of each day until his unkempt self would appear at the kitchen door for dinner with an uncanny sense of timing regardless of when we broke bread, which could vary from night to night. He typically had a dozen or so keys jangling from a ring on his belt, for what I had no idea, since beyond the van, he didn't appear to own anything that needed to be locked.

It seemed that most of McFire's possessions had fallen off the back of a truck. He was endlessly trying to interest visitors in buying cases of cassette tapes, silver plated dinner services, fondue sets, and such. We would not have been surprised if he whipped open his ragged great coat to reveal rows of watches.

McFire had long, greasy hair, which he tied in a ponytail, broad shoulders he boasted were a result of lifting weights in prison, and the first tattoo I'd seen not affixed to a sailor's biceps. He was so named by Jack because of his bad luck, which included a proclivity for starting fires in inappropriate places or letting them get out of control in appropriate places like our burn barrel, which he lit one day after pouring gasoline on the contents -- mostly paper and cardboard -- and nearly torched the outhouse.

He had his own lexicon: Water was *wooder*, anyhow was *anymore*, an asterisk was an *asterlick*, diarrhea was *dire rear*, and my fave -- his Polaroid camera was a *Paranoid*.

McFire's goal in life was to get to Las Vegas, which he eventually did after parading around in a cervical collar until he was able to weasel some insurance money from a whiplash claim based on a non-existent car crash. We later heard he had a job at a casino on the Vegas Strip. I pictured him with a regulation haircut bowing to biddies feeding one-armed bandits as he swept floors and emptied ashtrays. Alas, it turned out that McFire's big step up actually was a disimprovement, as he might say: We heard later still that bad luck had struck again. He was back in prison on an insurance fraud charge.

McFire had bonhomie to spare but no detectable common sense, once showing up at my place years later during a Christmas holiday with gifts for my then two- and four-year-old children. They were massive hunting knives that had probably fallen off the back of a truck.

Owen Owen was a beanpole of an Irishman with brilliant red hair and freckles. He had been bequeathed some money by an aunt and was spending it on seeing the U S of A. When the Trailways bus on which he was riding stopped in New Park, he got off.

A stroll up the main drag took him to the New Park Tavern. Doctor Duck was holding court on his captain's chair in the townie bar, and one thing led to another.

This included a suggestion that Owen Owen join us on an upcoming trip to the Florida Keys.

Doctor Duck had the annoying habit of inviting people to join us on trips that he almost inevitably backed out of at the last minute. After all, someone had to hose down those bar mats each morning. But Owen Owen, so named by Jack, of course, was a pleasure, a sweet and profoundly naive self-confessed virgin who, he said, had never been able to master unfastening brassieres and other rudiments of bedding a lass. He could not get over the fact that Americans drove everywhere, seldom walked anywhere, and drank their beer cold.

Owen Owen was one of the few interlopers who wasn't eventually encouraged to take a hike. He laughed at Jack's bad jokes and worst puns, listened dutifully as Jack read from his personal bible, a children's book titled *Things That Make Me Grouchy*, and assisted him in blowing cigarette smoke back in people's faces at the tavern with flashlights retrofitted by Jack with model airplane propellers.

My bus was full for the trip to the Keys. Jack had the flu and was running a fever, so he crawled to the back and onto the deck above the engine compartment where he fashioned a sweat lodge by wrapping himself in blankets.

Jack's fever broke in South Carolina, and he was once again his febrile self when we stopped at a Pancake House for breakfast. We crammed into a booth across from a table where some Jehovah's Witnesses were planning a day of going door-to-door peddling *The Watchtower* magazine.

One pun after another flowed from Jack's rejuvenated mind, including a groaner about time being fun for frogs when they're having flies, prompting Owen Owen to blow coffee through his nose, a few drops of which reached the Jehovahs' table. He blushed a deep red and apologized. They smiled thinly.

Achem, a friend of Jane's sister, was a German with an expired Green Card who aspired to be an artist. He showed up at a Flag Day party and as the weekend wound down, asked if he could stay on for a few days to do some landscape painting.

Within a few days, Jack was calling him "Ahem" to his face, making Van Gogh's ear jokes, and telling him to "Speak English, dammit" in an unsubtle effort to get him to scram, but Achem had no means to do so and no one he called would drive out and take him back to Philadelphia. Jack became so frustrated trying to understand what Achem was saying at dinner one night in his animated but badly fractured English, that he growled, pushed his plate away and bit a piece out of an edge of the octagonal table across from the bite mark Zarnie had left years earlier.

I finally drove Achem to the city after he beamingly unveiled the fruit of his labors -- a large painting in the Expressionist style of what vaguely resembled the long driveway and fields surrounding it. I hung the painting over the fireplace in the stereo room where it remained in all its hideousness until the farm ceased to be.

I didn't understand until later that Achem was desperately lonely. I also felt ashamed after learning from an acquaintance that he had told him we were the only Americans who were nice to him. This was just prior to him hanging himself by the neck in the stairway to the acquaintance's apartment.

I happened to be in the kitchen when the phone rang. The caller announced himself as L.R., whom I knew well as a malingerer who would drop in on his travels to freeload before moving on to freeload somewhere else.

He was at the bus station in New Park and needed a ride to the farm.

L.R. considered himself to be a proto-bohemian. He had grown his hair long, smoked marijuana and claimed that was into Ginsberg and Kerouac long before others. I considered him to be a supercilious asshole with a smile as thin as November ice. We did not hit it off. Twice, he put his hand on my leg during the ride to the farm and twice I removed it. L.R. finally got the hint when I told him he was welcome to get out and walk back to town.

I was building a picnic table, and when we arrived at the farm I asked him to give me a hand carrying boards from the barn. He said he was tired from his travels and retired to a hammock in the back yard to nap. This he did most afternoons.

Then there was L.R.'s attire, typically a loincloth under a long shirt or tunic, and sometimes just a loincloth arranged in such a way that one or, if you were really unlucky, both of his testicles were visible. He said he had become a disciple of a yogi (I wondered whether if it was Snatchabanana) and boasted that he was living an ascetic's life. Apparently except when he drank our beer and smoked our pot, which he did in copious quantities.

He had a mean streak. There was a large web that a spider had artfully woven between two tree trunks above the upper garden. It would glisten like strands of jewels in the morning dew. I would fill a mug with coffee and hike up to the web on sunny mornings to marvel at the masterwork of a creature I never once saw. Knowing that I liked the web, L.R. made a show of walking through it in my presence one day. Later on, I noticed a swollen spot developing on his left shoulder. It was a spider bite.

I don't recall how Luther came into our lives. He may have been left behind -- willingly or otherwise -- after a Flag Day party.

Luther ran about 6-foot-7 and had a magnificent physique he had been unable to capitalize on. He was preternaturally shy. With Pattie's gentle encouragement, his story emerged in bits and pieces: He had been a star basketball player at a New York City high school who was recruited by major college programs, got a full ride out of poverty and a broken home to a big Midwestern university, but could not adjust to campus life, which for him was like trying to survive on an alien planet. He said he dropped out before the first basketball practice and was ashamed to go back to the city.

Luther spent much of each day wandering the yard and fields. He said he never had pets growing up, and I marveled at his love of our critters, who in ways unfathomable to me always knew when they had encountered a two-legged soul mate. A cat would amble across the yard and, tail erect, weave figure eights between Luther's ankles. He would reach down -- this always seemed to take forever because he did nothing quickly -- to greet the cat, now standing on its hind legs, who would rub its head against massive hands that no longer palmed basketballs.

Like I said, one of the biggest lies told about the farm was that it was a commune.

This resulted in hilarity at the richly deserved expense of a writer from a national magazine who was doing a story on the communal farms that then were ubiquitous in rural Pennsylvania, New York and West Virginia. The writer would not be put off when she called from New Park and I told her Kiln Farm was just a plain old farm. She insisted on seeing the place and meeting our "leader."

Someone, probably Doctor Duck, had ratted out the farm's location. She said she and a photographer would be arriving within the hour. "You're really wasting your time," I told her when she pulled up, but she waved my remark aside.

"Why don't you show me around, then introduce me to your leader?" she suggested to Doctor Doc and myself.

"Well, our leader is actually very shy," Doc explained. "She hasn't spoken a word in years."

"Oh!" the writer exclaimed. "A woman is your leader?"

She was excited, I suppose, because men were typically the "leaders" of communes and she thought she had herself a scoop.

A tour of the grounds and garden commenced. The photographer snapped pictures while the writer asked questions the consistency of pabulum. We eventually returned to the house where the audience with our "leader" could not be put off any longer.

Writer and photographer were led into the kitchen and thence to the Phone Booth. Doc pointed to the door.

"Our leader's in there," he deadpanned. "You can only have a few minutes with her."

"Only a few minutes?" the writer asked.

"Aye-aye," Doc replied.

When the writer opened the door, our "leader" was revealed to be Lobelia, regal in the Wagnerian horned helmet atop her head and a purple cape draped over her back.

Lobes chewed her cud. The writer screamed and fled, the photographer not far behind her.

"Maah!" Lobes bleated. "Maaaaah!"

CHAPTER TWELVE

*"Don't bogart that joint, my friend,
pass it over to me."*

  The impulsive Jack proudly announced one spring day that while we were all off somewhere or other, he had dug a pond for the ducks with a backhoe Hawk had trailered to the farm in the losing battle to fill in ever deepening ruts in the long driveway. The pond was a hit with the ducks, but was situated a mere 10 feet or so from the back wall of the house. It soon turned the color of café au lait, quickly became an open sewer awash in duck poop, and threatened to undermine the house's iffy foundation.

  Jack filled in the pond.

  Jack's next impulsive act was to plant marijuana a bit later that spring, again when everyone was away from

Kiln Farm. It was inevitable that we would have done so sooner or later. This is because pretty much our only out-of-pocket expenses were beer, toilet paper and pot, the latter being costly in the quantities we smoked even back in those halcyon days of the nickel bag.

Jack never did anything halfway, and sowed four or five 30-foot rows with marijuana seeds at the outset of a summer that turned out be ideal for pot cultivation: It was fairly wet early on as the seeds germinated and grew, and endlessly sunny with ample humidity later on as the plants matured.

He at least had the foresight to plant the seeds behind several rows of corn, but the marijuana soon outpaced the corn in the fertile soil, and had the pot not been at the upper reaches of the garden, it would have been visible from the back yard and short driveway. As it was, the sight of dozens of plants doing the distinctive marijuana hula in a breeze -- and no other form of vegetation except bamboo has so seductive a motion -- was worrisome when viewed from my vantage point in the attic.

While some of us would later become pretty good at sexing pot plants -- females produce flowers and hence buds that contain the psychoactive metabolite that gets you high, while males just take up space -- no one realized the first year that the males should be pulled so they did not cross pollinate the females. Of course, this is exactly what happened, so what we got was an enormous quantity of pot without a single bud of consequence.

As Doctor Doc, summoning a word from his rich vocabulary, put it, "The harvest was nugatory."

After being pulled, dried in the shed loft and then stripped, the leaves filled a half dozen five-gallon plastic buckets, all but one of which was buried in the ground around the farm. That one was secreted under the earth floor of the shed.

We could get stoned on our first harvest, but it took joints the size of a pinky finger to do so. Jack called these monstrosities Zeppelins because of their resemblance to the German airships.

The second year's marijuana crop was only slightly more potent despite efforts to weed out the male plants. This gave Bigfoot an idea that could have blown him to where Pattie and little Caitlin were to go.

As a laboratory technician, Bigfoot had amassed a considerable quantity of discarded glassware, including beakers, flasks and piping. He rigged a complicated apparatus over a hot plate in the farm's long disused original outhouse that looked like a Magdeburg hemisphere, only made of glass, that was heated with highly volatile laboratory alcohol. This device bubbled away over several days, eventually cooking down a five-gallon bucket of marijuana leaves into a dark grease-like substance with the consistency of Moroccan hashish.

The result was two one-quart Mason jars filled with this primordial slime-like grease, sacrilegiously described by Jack as a reverse Miracle of the Loaves. Bigfoot was given the honor of smoking the first bowl in Davis's mortar shell pipe. After several tries, he got the grease going, inhaled a big chestful, held his breath for a few seconds and then exhaled explosively.

"Jesus!" he exclaimed.

And so this potent concoction became known as Jesus Grease.

Our efforts to brew beer were desultory, while our lone winemaking caper ended with a bang.

The beer lacked a certain something -- taste, I suppose -- and was exiled to the cellar until a winter night when there was an ice storm, the roads were impassable and, horror or horrors, we . . . ran . . . out . . . of . . . beer. Up came a dust-covered case of this slumgullion of a home brew, which had been decanted into Löwenbräu Oktoberfest bottles and capped. It was undrinkable, but we drank it anyway.

When you have dandelions, you make dandelion wine, or so Bess said. This she did in a big glass water cooler bottle. The wine was lugged down into the cellar to age, Bess and her kids moved on, and we forgot about it. Two years or so had gone by. It was a fall evening when the setting sun angled just so into the kitchen and across the octagonal table. All was right with the world. Unless we were having lentil loaf. I don't recall.

This pastorale was suddenly broken by a loud noise in the cellar that was part *kaboom!* and part *whoosh!* Or maybe it was *whoosh! kaboom!* I was first to the cellar door, which I opened slowly and with trepidation while desperately trying to recall where I had last seen the fire extinguisher.

It was raining in the cellar. At least it sounded like rain. A rain of dandelion wine that had gone supernova in the big bottle, blown the cork and erupted all over the walls and ceiling.

In addition to goat's head soup, with the Jamaicans came lamb's bread, a potent high-grade strain of marijuana said to be the favorite of Bob Marley and his band.

The farm's first two harvests were to lamb's bread what a bicycle with training wheels is to a Porsche, but within a couple years of the arrival of Marley's extended family, we were growing pretty decent pot with their seed stock and advice. From then on out, the harvests were anything but nugatory and Zeppelins were history.

Adapting Jamaican growing methods and mindful of destructive deer and woodchucks, who love nibbling on marijuana plants, we planted seedlings in camouflaged buckets filled with topsoil from the garden, and snugged them in the crooks of trees along the upper edge of the garden where they were out of reach of fuds. Dragging around a stepladder to water these plants was a pain, but they got plenty of sun although hidden behind foliage, and probably not even the keenest eyed observer would have noticed them.

The harvest was considerably smaller than the first two years, but the yield was sensational: Dozens of potent buds, some the size and shape of Michelob beer bottles, that glistened, were incredibly pungent, sticky to the touch and deeply intoxicating. Just like lamb's bread.

Doc harvested his annual crop of honey at the end of the first summer of bucket cultivation. As he did each year, he took a sample down to the ag college at the university in New Park where his faculty adviser, who was an expert in determining the provenance of the plants on which bees feast, would take a taste and declare that the source of the honey was thus and such a tree or plant. This time the professor was baffled.

"Well, it's not from fruit trees. Or wildflowers," he opined. "I've never tasted honey quite like this."

Doc did not let on, and the secret of our marijuana-suffused honey remained between us and the bees.

We never got into trouble growing pot and as naive as it may seem looking back, I believe the reason is that we never tried to make money from it. And were plain lucky. Nor did we sell any other kind of drug. This vocation had terminated the brief stay of a housemate when Dadd found bottles of prescription pain killers he was selling in New Park.

We did, however, give a fair amount of pot away, and the payback for our generosity was large.

King Mike was a master mechanic who kept the Troy-Bilt rototiller and our two Gravely walk-behind lawn mowers in tune. Ed was a welder and would repair the tiller and mowers when big stuff on them broke. It was he who fabricated Dadd's oil drum grill. Richard was a contractor who would take away the dregs of our motor pool on his flatbed truck. Dick was a sportsman and hunter who gifted us venison and fish. Hack was a tree surgeon who felled, cut and trucked in dead trees, adding substantially to our wood pile. Thomas was a bricklayer who bought the materials and built a chimney to better vent the wood stove. Larry was the blacksmith who shod Dude. Ricardo was the New Park Tavern executive chef who cooked at later Flag Day parties and on other occasions gifted us bushel baskets of freshly-caught Maryland blue crabs. Victor was a ceramicist who in gratitude for being welcome to come by and toke up, which his wife forbade him to do at home, donated an oddball assemblage of ceramic pieces about four feet tall. We installed what came to be known as The Victor next to the front porch steps. It seemed to get uglier by the year but then began to fall apart, many of its bits eventually returning to the elements as they disappeared into the earth on which the sculpture sat.

It was inevitable that some of the rougher examples of the Jamaican experience would find their way to the farm. They were Jamaica Miles and Joel.

Miles, who wasn't particularly straight about anything, was actually from the Bahamas. He had movie star good looks and was a counterfeiter by trade, while Joel, who was Jamaican and the largest person I've ever met who didn't wear a football uniform, was his bodyguard and driver. Once Joel was squared away about where his handgun should go when he and Miles visited -- in the glove box of their BMW 700 series and not tucked into his dungarees -- things went fine.

Miles and Joel would spend part of each winter in Florida where Joel introduced us to the joys of picking psilocybin mushrooms. They would sometimes tag along as we made the rounds of summer parties at Kiln Farm wannabes, and there were several farms that aspired to be like us. Or better than us, whatever that was. This led to an unwelcome sort of unreciprocated competition that took several forms, including which farm had the most awesome bonfire. This was strange because we never had a bonfire at our parties.

Most obnoxiously competitive was Unicorn Hollow, a farm owned by Scully, who had made his nut wholesaling janitorial products only to take a powder when he invested his fortune in marketing a reusable marijuana cigarette. Alas, the world was not ready for a reusable marijuana cigarette, let alone one that resembled a small tampon. And probably still isn't.

Scully thought he could impress us -- and it was clear that his target was the laid back crew from the farm, which included Miles, Joel and Bart on this particular day -- by arranging for a buddy who was a pilot in an Air National Guard helicopter unit to do a fly-in when the ritual bonfire got blazing. The chopper of choice was a UH-1 Huey, a machine ubiquitous with Nam.

This profoundly lame-brained idea at first subtly, then more loudly and then deafeningly asserted itself with the distinctive *thunk, thunk, thunk* of the Huey's rotor blades as the chopper set down in a field next to a party chockablock with veterans, some of them not too stable to begin with and others not too stable and tripping. Some succumbed to flashbacks, panicked and fled. Scully got busted and the chopper pilot got court martialed. Served them right.

Then there was the Last Rezort, which began hosting Halloween parties about the time we lost our taste for them. Wilbo, who usually was this farm's sole resident, never tried to compete with us. It would never have occurred to his gentle self. The main attraction at

Wilbo's parties was a massive non-competitive bonfire with a twist: People were asked to bring castoff furniture to throw into the flames. There was also the occasional television set, which would explode to the cheers of the stoned and drunken horde.

The farm's chief would-be rival was Scylla Tryst, which was presumably named after Scylla, the mythological Greek she-dragon. The highlights of this summer party were a tug-of-war and the obligatory bonfire. Sally, the Type A she-dragon who dominated Scylla Tryst, would stack her tug-of-war team with ringers, but never came close to winning, especially with Joel, our own ringer, on the righteous end of the rope.

Jack built the bonfire at Sally's behest for what turned out to be her last party. "Make it bigger! Make it bigger!" she implored him as he threw on more and more wood. The bonfire soon threatened to roar out of control. Fire trucks summoned by neighbors arrived, Sally dissolved into paroxysms of tears, and had to be sedated.

The sassafras tree notwithstanding, I didn't spend much time thinking about what farm life might have been like 200 years ago. But my imagination sometimes did wander way back when I sat in the stereo room with its deeply recessed windows and substantial fireplace, pretty much unchanged from when the original part of the house was built. One interior wall of the fireplace still included the hinge works for a swiveling spit from which an iron pot probably hung.

  Light from the late-afternoon sun would slant just so into the room in winter -- it was quite lovely -- and in my imagination I would sort of smell salt cured meat from an animal the menfolk from the earliest Van der Killen generations had trapped or shot. There would be fresh hearth baked bread, sugared peaches for dessert, a whiff of pipe tobacco, and a staple like turnip and leek soup bubbling in the pot as firelight magnified the shadows, tallow candle flames bent because of a drafty window. Perhaps there were a couple of big dogs warming themselves on a rug near the fireplace; I hoped so.

  Miles and Joel never became acclimated to winter weather, and we would get a roaring blaze going in that fireplace when they called to say they were coming by.

  The thermometer was playing footsie with zero one evening. Dadd, Jack, Miles, Joel, another guest and I sat on the floor in front of the fire in a semi circle, listening to reggae and passing around a massive spliff Joel had rolled of lamb's bread and cigarette tobacco. It was not exactly a Colonial Era scene. The fire drew me in, as fires always had from summer camp and my parent's house when I would lie on my stomach on the living room carpet when my father would get a fire going in our fieldstone fireplace on special occasions like Thanksgiving and Christmas.

As the joint became smaller, the smoke grew thicker. The flames from the fireplace were a mesmerizing yellow, blue and green. I suddenly came to my senses and considered getting up before I hyperventilated, but was unable to move. At that moment, Dadd did hyperventilate and fell forward toward the hearth. He was grabbed by Joel just in time to keep him from whacking his head.

CHAPTER THIRTEEN

"Eight miles high and when you touch down
You'll find that it's stranger than known"

Most of my psychedelic adventures ended on pretty much the same note: The welcome feeling of coming down after 10 or 12 hours, or sometimes even longer, followed by blessed sleep. But the outset of each trip was always different.

My first trip -- on LSD -- got under way as I was staring into a plate of eggs and hash brown potatoes at a greasy spoon at the shore and wondering why the things I had been told would happen when I tripped, weren't happening. As if on cue, the eggs and spuds began boogalooing. I left them uneaten and hastened down to the beach with Jack, sometime lover Paige and a couple of Jack's buds from Nam. I stood in the surf, the water lapping at my ankles. It felt like I was standing on the rim of the world. A formation of pelicans flew overhead like aircraft on submarine patrol. They were the last even vaguely coherent thoughts I would have for hours.

  I had thrice been saved from drowning by my companions when I wandered further into the surf, and once from being hit by a car when I tried to cross a busy highway to get back to Jack's car. Or so I was told the next day as I realized that I had dived head first into the deep end of the psychedelic pool.

  Lysergic acid diethylamide was the Kiln Farm trip of choice, but by no means the only kind of trip we did. LSD is a synthetic version of two natural consciousness alterers -- psilocybin, which we did a fair amount of in the form of so-called magic mushrooms, and mescaline. The latter I did only a few times as it was among the hardest to buy trip early in the decade and impossible to find later on.

  Sandoz Laboratories had synthesized LSD in 1961. It first came to public attention when bad boy Harvard professors Timothy Leary and Richard Alpert invited graduate students and friends to drop acid with them under the veneer-thin pretext of scholarship. Alpert later became all spiritual, changed his name to Ram Dass, and penned *Be Here Now*, a fuzzy but plausible and nicely written synthesis of yoga, spirituality and meditation that became a counterculture classic. Novelist Ken Kesey and his Merry Pranksters, celebrated in Tom Wolfe's *The Electric Cool Aid Acid Test*, were also in the vanguard, but didn't pretend they were tripping for anything other than the sheer pleasure of it.

The LSD we dropped usually was very clean, whether blotter, gelatin squares, orange sunshine, barrels or liquid-laced sugar cubes. This is because we got into acid fairly early. As the decade went on and demand soared, it became more difficult to find trips that were not contaminated and consequentially dicey because of impurities.

The outset of some trips was gradual in the extreme. You didn't feel any different and your surroundings hadn't changed, but speech patterns became subtly and then noticeably altered. If you were hanging outdoors with a companion or two admiring the scenery, the conversation went something like this as the trip commenced:

"Look at the alfafa blowing in the breeze. Lovely."

"Yeah, and the sunlight is striking the heads just so."

"And look at the bees. They're grittle buckle gumping all blover yee-oh."

"Yup, grittle buckle gump gumping buckle snork weeeeee!"

You had a preternaturally vivid awareness of your surroundings while tripping -- in this instance somehow seeing each individual alfalfa head although there were many thousands -- and everyday objects were transformed. On one trip I saw a goose neck-shaped section of white PVC pipe in a junk pile out of the corner of my eye. I thought it was a swan. On a few occasions, an observed conversation suddenly lapsed into silence as if the soundtrack to a film had failed, only to resume a short time later, while a friend sometimes would respond to something a person had said although they hadn't said anything.

I am grateful that I had hands to hold on my first trip. I was to return the favor many times over once I understood that only the most phantasmagorical trips rendered me incapable of walking, talking and driving to hospital emergency rooms.

My first trip of the ER kind occurred during the second Flag Day party when Bigfoot walked off the kitchen porch with a plastic cup of beer in each hand, didn't realize he had run out of porch, and crashed onto a slate walk, splitting open his forehead. It somehow fell to me to drive him to the hospital although I was tripping my brains out.

The ER was standing room only, and the soundtrack to my trip became coughs, hacks, wails, sirens and ear-splitting public address announcements. It took about two hours before the Bigfoot's number came up and he got his head stitched back together. It only seemed interminable.

My second trip of the ER kind occurred one of the few times I tripped indoors and the only time I tripped in the dead of winter. It figured.

In a repeat of the Flag Day incident, Tim, a guy whose wife had thrown him out of their house earlier that day, became so zonked that he was in his bare feet although the temperature was below freezing when he walked off the kitchen porch, didn't realize that he had run out of porch, and went ass over tea kettle onto the ice-slicked walk, splitting open *his* forehead. He was in no condition to drive, so it of course fell to me to take him to the ER.

I find it difficult to convey the horror of negotiating icy country roads in the middle of the night while experiencing acid rushes with someone lying in the back of my bus alternately moaning and threatening to throw up. Still, we were in and out of the ER in no time. It only seemed interminable.

It was a torrid late summer afternoon, lethargy had descended on the farm like an invisible fog, and we were sweating like pigs. There was only one thing to do: Drop acid and go to the creek.

Going to the creek used to be as easy as walking through the cornfield below the front porch. There we would splash about with Bart, who loved the water, in a not-that-deep pool behind Zarnie's dam, but the creek eventually became a rivulet and the pool silted in. The next best thing was much better -- a larger and deeper pool on a creek in a woods about four miles from the farm.

The pool was our secret, or so we thought until the day a bunch of people showed up from Scylla Tryst who thought the pool was *their* secret.

This stretch of creek ran over and between boulders, visitors from the last Ice Age that had stayed put after the big thaw. One boulder was broad enough for several people to sunbathe on and angled into the water in such a way that you could dip your feet in the water or slide all the way in. Parts of the pool were deeper than I am tall. I'm 6-foot-2, so the pool was a bit more than a fathom, as Jack put it in nautical parlance, while some of the boulders had been conveniently eroded in such a way that you could sit on them and be submerged up to your neck.

Best of all, the creek ran high, fast, clean and cool even during the driest summers, the water furiously boiling over the rocks, and was perfumed by wildflowers along its banks. The spot was especially magical on summer evenings when we would skinny dip, and if we listened closely, could hear the melancholy sound of whistles as they carried several miles up the creek from trains rattling through the crossing next to the New Park Tavern.

There was an iron ring about five inches in diameter hammered into the broad boulder, which the locals called David's Rock, or alternately The Rock That David Sat On. The ring had been used by yeomen many years earlier to tie their wagons while they were lowered into the creek in a primitive version of a car wash. Or perhaps car washes are modern versions of wagon washes.

David was the ghost of a boy by that name who had been swept away during a hurricane and was occasionally seen, so the locals claimed, sitting in a semi-transparent state on the rock where he pined for his family.

The acid of choice this day was clean, powerful, but not too powerful, and trippy, but not wildly hallucinatory. One by one we slid into the creek, paddled about and then settled onto the boulder benches. I cooled down and my mind expanded as I breathed in the wildflower perfume.

I closed my eyes, let the acid transport me for a while before returning to the here and now, and opening my eyes. To my right, only Jack's eyes and forehead were visible above the water. Like the head of a big, hairy toad. Same for Jane and Hawk, who were on the far bank of the creek. Then there was Bart, neck deep in the water to my left with his eyes rolled back.

Good dog!

The incongruous piece of furniture was tucked into a dark corner of the stereo room: One of those five-foot-high blue nitrous oxide tanks you once saw in dentists' offices. We had put a lamp shade over the valve works in a laughable effort to camouflage the tank.

Our infatuation with laughing gas, instigated by sampling the nitrous-filled balloons you could buy in parking lots at Grateful Dead concerts, lasted only a few weeks, or a couple of tanks worth. During that time nary a visitor gave our weird piece of furniture a second glance.

Nitrous causes dizziness and euphoria and elevates music to higher levels of enjoyment, in our experience almost anything by Pink Floyd and David Sancious's *Forest of Feelings*, a rock-fusion album of that time. But nitrous has a serious downside: the higher you become, the more common sense abandons you. That meant bad things could happen. And did.

A friend in New Park who gifted us the tanks later fell down two flights of stairs after over inhaling. He found Jesus on the first floor landing and never did nitrous or any other kind of drug again.

The fleeting nitrous era at the farm came to a crashing end late one night. I was drifting off to sleep when I heard someone come in the kitchen door. It was Tim. I heard him walk into the stereo room, then the *whoosh!* of the tank valve being opened and the sound of a plastic trash bag -- our nitrous delivery system of choice -- being filled with gas, which Tim then put over his head and inhaled. A minute or so later there was a sickening *thunk*. Tim had broken the cardinal rule of nitrous consumption: Standing up. He fell into the tank and the tank in turn fell onto him. He split open his forehead, a precursor of what was to happen on that frigid night a couple of years later.

Nitrous suddenly didn't seem so cool.

Zarnie had journeyed to a desert in the Southwest from Colorado where he picked peyote buttons, filled a shirt box-sized package with them, and mailed the box to the farm care of me a few weeks before the first Flag Day party. The buttons' potent juices had eaten through several layers of plastic wrap and aluminum foil, and the bottom of the box was noticeably sticky when the postmaster handed it to me. Fearing that federal drug agents might be about to pounce, I kept looking in the rear view mirror of my bus driving back to the farm, but no one had suspected anything.

You can't just pop peyote buttons in your mouth and chew your way to Nirvana. They are spineless cacti that produce an edible fruit, but a consumer is well advised to remove the ring of white fuzz from the middle of each button. This is because the fuzz contains strychnine, which is poisonous. Then you have to dry the buttons, which I did in a fruit dryer in the wood shop. Then you have to grind the buttons, which I did with an antique hand-cranked coffee mill that Hawk had picked up at an auction. Then you have to put the ground buttons in a drinkable medium, in my case a goats milkshake-like concoction that we drank out of double shot glasses stolen from the New Park Tavern.

Peyote can cause intense nausea even after it is cleaned, although leavening it with goats milk helped ease the urge to heave whatever was in your stomach. Potency varies substantially between buttons and because of the time lag from when the buttons are ingested and when tripping commences.

Psilocybin mushrooms produce a high not unlike LSD, although one that is not quite so sharp edged, which is to say more forgiving.

They are best consumed fresh, which in our case entailed low crawling into a pasture near Jamaica Miles' South Florida condo at the crack of dawn to pick them off cow pies.

Late one winter we went foraging on a homebound trip from the Keys and collected a big bag of mushrooms. We continued our way north after stopping at a fireworks shop and fruit stand on the Tamiami Trail to buy fireworks and bushel bags of oranges and grapefruit. This was the mid-1970s and a few stretches of Interstate 95 still had not been completed in Georgia. We were driving well below the speed limit through a one-stoplight town early the next morning when we were pulled over. I'm sure that was a coincidence and had nothing to do with my bus's colorful flower curtains and the Grateful Dead sticker prominently displayed in the back window.

The sheriff's deputies, who were straight out of Central Casting, told us to get out of the bus. As we stood shivering in the chill and our thoughts turned to chain gangs and prison rape, the deputies -- one gangly tall and the other pudgy short -- looked through everything in the bus, came to the bag containing the mushrooms, shined their flashlights into it, had no idea what they were looking at, probably thinking it was some kind of organic hippie crap food, and closed the bag. Then they found the fireworks, which they confiscated before sending us on our very relieved way.

I am a frequent and vivid dreamer who can remember some, but by no means all of my dreams. These dreams are typically mosaics of fragments of the past and future, are rarely nightmarish, seldom erotic and typically mundane, although I have the gift of tongues when dreaming and am able to comprehend what people are saying no matter the language. These nocturnal journeys often have soundtracks, sometimes music that I recently listened to with no apparent connection to the dream, and seem to have been selected by a mad deejay. I always dream in color, and agree with the view I read somewhere that changing where one sleeps results in more interesting dreams. This was the case on the rare occasions when I slept in my old bed at my parent's house, or even rarer occasions when the weather was so awful on travels that I'd spring for a motel room rather than sleep in my VW bus.

  Some of my dreams are frustration dreams -- not being able to find my bus in a labyrinth of dark and forbidding inner city streets, and in later years not being able to call a loved one because my cell phone is in pieces and I can't put it back together. Some dreams involve people and places I have known, although the people are in places different than where I knew them and the places are conglomerations of, say, the farmhouse, a rustic high street bookshop in England and a fishing village in Japan that I knew from my waking life.

  While my psychedelic adventures have informed these dreams, I don't remember dreaming following a trip with one exception that was unforgettable well after the fact. I dreamed I was wandering somewhere, although I didn't have a clue as to where at the time. The temperature was Sahara hot. An exquisite waterfall appeared. It was tucked into a small canyon with a few cottonwood trees and, of all things, a reliquary with a statue of the Virgin Mary. There were fresh cut flowers at her feet.

As anyone who has done a fair amount of LSD will tell you, the more times you trip, the less powerful the drug is, and indeed my trips were to become far less visual, which is to say hallucinatory, as time went on. This eventually led me to drop dropping acid. After all, why put up with the rushes and sometime other unpleasantnesses if there weren't hallucinations?

Early on, however, I was hallucinating like crazy, and one day tripped alone for the first time. I wandered past the shed into the field where Bart would woof at the moon and sat down. I was overwhelmed by visuals. It felt as if I were in an airliner flying through pockets of turbulence with no seat belt to hold me down, while my only tie to the temporal world was the sweat running from my armpits and down my sides. The sweat felt strangely cold although the afternoon was warm.

I laid on my back and looked up. The pearlescent clouds raced faster and faster. I had the sensation of there being a symphonic overture to a great event that was about to unfold, which I later deduced was a snippet from Antonioni's *Zabriskie Point*. I had bought the soundtrack album to the movie, which was vaguely about the 1960s counterculture, because it included "Love Scene," a beautifully simple Jerry Garcia guitar solo. (I eventually saw *Zabriskie Point* at an art house in New Park. It was awful.)

Then a massive draft horse tawny gold in color galloped out of the clouds, its muscular sinews, broad back, powerful hindquarters and long mane glistening in the sun as I pressed myself into the ground. The field became cloaked in shadow as it approached, silently galloped overhead and was gone. I was terrified.

That horse began visiting me in my dreams a few years ago, which begs the question of whether it is possible to have acid flashbacks while sleeping.

I thought I only tripped for the heck of it until I recently reread some of my journals from my time at the farm. In retrospect, they were embarrassing piffle for the most part. One especially egregious entry reads, "Gloomy Saturday weather takes my head and like a basketball dribbles it up and down, up and down, up and down." But it is obvious from some entries that I sometimes tripped to try to unlock a sort of alembic of creative thought.

Did I succeed? More or less. For one thing, I concluded, as greater minds had long before me, you can only dream that which exists. For another, my life has been deeply informed by my trips and better for them. As I wrote in one journal entry, "After you do acid, everything has a little bit of acid in it."

I never had a bad trip, merely an occasional one -- typically on high-powered LSD -- that was less than enjoyable because the environment or the company, or both, weren't quite right. (My draft horse experience was not a bad trip by any means, merely a very intense one.) I sometimes would lose a pair of shoes while tripping or not be able to figure out afterwards why I had sand between my toes. But there never was the feeling of alienation, anxiety or paranoia, let alone the sheer terror, that people sometimes felt while tripping who ended up in a fetal ball in a corner, their universe collapsed in on them, with friends holding their hands and trying to talk them down. "It's all right. We're your friends. You're cool. It'll be over before you know it."

I had an antipathy toward getting physical while tripping with the conspicuous exception of 3,4-

Methylenedioxyamphetamine, a psychedelic better known as MDA.

MDA was gentle and nicknamed the Love Drug because it made you want to hug the nearest person. Or a lamp post. Or anything. And back in the early 1970s, even ponder whether that Tricky Dick wasn't such a bad chap after all. Making love on MDA was sensational, with even the smallest caress imparting a feeling of profundity, and main events . . . well, imparting a feeling of really profound profundity. I enjoyed this kind of trip so much that I bought an ounce of the pinkish powder for $200. That ounce begat easy-to-digest gelatin capsules which I filled with a McDonald's milkshake thingy that had a teensy spoon on one end. Although I never kept track, I am sure that a hundred or so people enjoyed that ounce over the couple of years it took to consume it.

Then there was a Halloween party in the back room of the New Park Tavern where George Thorogood and the Destroyers played. We filled a baby bottle usually used for nursing newborn goats with red wine and laced it with a big dollop of MDA. The bottle was passed around on the dance floor and dozens of people took a suck or two, unaware that they were soon going to become comfortably numb.

That Halloween night notwithstanding, the worst thing anyone can do with trips are psychedelic assassinations; that is, dropping acid or another powerful trip into the drink of an unsuspecting victim. MDA was different. It is a sad coda to our experience that Ecstasy, a close relative chemically to MDA with an identical high, was vilified years later following breathless, if false, media reports about pernicious traits it didn't have, and criminal behavior it didn't cause in its users.

MDA is a federal Schedule One drug along with heroin and cocaine, and most stupidly, marijuana, as well. American society remains profoundly hypocritical when it comes to marijuana use, even for palliative medical purposes. It also condemns substantially harmless mind expanders such as MDA and Ecstacy that have proven to be valuable in research and therapy for Post Traumatic Stress Disorder, among other psychiatric conditions bedeviling our modern minds. Meanwhile, prescription ups and downs are abused by the billions, including the very scolds who would have insisted that we be busted for tripping. Had that happened, some of us would probably still be doing time.

Then there were self-inflicted psychedelic assassinations.

Doctor Duck had a brother Raymond (never ever call him Ray, okay?), an imperious fitness freak, who would drive out to the farm to take extended jogs around the fields. On rare occasions, he would partake of a beer. Pot and psychedelics were beneath his dignity.

Raymond ran up to the kitchen porch one afternoon in matching sweatshirt, pants and headband long before such ensembles became *de rigueur* for the fashion-conscious jogger. Jack had mixed a pitcher of orange juice suffused with acid that was being passed around. Raymond grabbed the pitcher as he continued to jog in place and chugged most of the contents as Jack sputtered, "Ray, Ray, you're drinking orange juice laced with LSD!"

A crazed look crossed Ray's face. "Laced with what?"

Two days later, he still was wandering wild eyed around the fields.

CHAPTER FOURTEEN

*"It's winter in America and ain't nobody fighting
'cause nobody knows what to save"*

The pace at Kiln Farm slowed during cold weather months and that was just fine.

Milking continued, but dairy goats are on a yearly cycle and their output dropped dramatically in the weeks before they came into heat with the spring thaw and were bred. Egg production decreased by about two thirds and the dogs -- except for Ged, the Great Pyrenees who was not bothered by the cold -- migrated from the kitchen porch to the slate pad under the wood stove. I don't know how they avoided frying their brains.

The water spigots and wellhead pump down in the milk house were wrapped with heat tape. Sometimes that wasn't enough, and they had to be thawed with a hair dryer. A couple of splashes of apple cider vinegar were added to the goats' water buckets to keep them from freezing. In extremely cold weather, there would be no running water in the house, so we had to lug buckets up to the kitchen to wash dishes with water heated on the gas stove, and to the bathroom to prime the toilet so it would flush. Showers were out.

Winter was a time for talking long walks. The fields fallow and trees bare, most of the birds having fled South and many critters in hibernation, the farm was stripped back to the basics. Shell, Pattie and I would set out from the farmhouse with the dogs -- bored and anxious for an adventure -- and Terrapin in tow.

Black crows heralded our intrusion on their turf with raucous caw-caws as they wheeled and careered, their black plumage so black that it appeared to be deep purple (great name for a prog rock group, right?) in the sunlight. We crunched our way across the fields, stopping at the turn on the long driveway to stand under the massive sycamore, which somehow seemed even larger when bereft of leaves, to confirm there still was a trickle of water from the underground spring flowing up and under the ice. The dogs would paw at the ice to try to get to the water. We would continue on, Terrapin inevitably falling behind and tiring, mewp-

mewping piteously until he was picked up and plopped onto one of our shoulders.

Snow had a cleansing effect, and anything rutted, muddy or rusted took on a respectable, if not exactly virginal, white. The view from the farmhouse roof after a snow was exhilarating. One moonless January night, we hoisted Doctor Duck's big telescope through The Hatch To The Universe in Vi's bedroom. Our objective was to spot Comet Kohoutek, which was supposed to blaze a fiery path through the southern sky. The comet did no such thing from our northerly vantage point, but the following month we finally saw it in the Florida Keys. It was a disappointing pinprick of light with a hair-thin tail.

Doctor Duck lectured endlessly on many subjects, and occasionally had something worthwhile to say. Through him, I became interested in sky watching as he taught me the procession of the moon, stars and planets, and how to identify the signs of the Zodiac. Aries, Taurus, Gemini, Cancer, Leo, Virgo, Libra, Scorpio and Sagittarius became my heavenly companions as they moved into view in spring, summer and fall, while Capricorn, Aquarius and Pisces -- which is my sign -- remained elusive because of where the farm was located in relation to that heavenly procession.

Eclipses were special times, and while the birds were tucked in for the night when the moon would go into eclipse, solar eclipses were another matter. One total solar eclipse was notable for its effect on the chickens, ducks, geese, peafowl and Percy.

These critters knew that the eclipse was imminent before we did, and one by one settled onto the lawn, or wherever they were, as the moon began to pass between the sun and earth. Although it was mid afternoon, there was an eerie stillness during the totality. It was only as the moon had moved away from the sun's face an hour or so later that the birds stirred.

Doctor Duck also introduced me to the medicinal power of herbs, primarily through *Culpepper's Herbal*, a 17th century pharmaceutical compendium. I have followed its advice over the years whether for a rare cough or fever.

There was a place we named the Magic Gardens.

This was once the 300-acre playground of a long-dead multimillionaire industrialist on the banks of a river not far from New Park. We used to navigate down by canoe under full moons.

The river wasn't passable when it iced up, but other times we would put several canoes into the river about a half mile above the gardens late in the evening when the moon was well up, and let the current take us down to a stone abutment where we would stash the canoes and tip-toe up into a magnificent series of terraced gardens. They were patrolled by elderly watchmen.

The gardens were a mix of Greco-Roman architecture and statuary, and some amazing topiary. The centerpiece was a reflecting pool in the middle of what was called the Long Walk where jets shot water into the air. The jets were off on our nocturnal visits, and the moonlit walk would be beautifully reflected in the pool.

There were subterranean rooms and a marble altar, as well as two massive iron pots, each large enough for a half dozen people to climb into. Which is exactly what happened one night when we heard a watchman approaching. We were all tripping, of course, and a woman friend we had brought along had to be muffled to stifle her laughter as the watchman ambled by whistling "Danny Boy."

Our navy was launched when Hawk bought a box of captain's hats with shiny black brims and gold anchors at an auction. He then bought a pickup load of truck tire inner tubes at another auction that we inflated and I stenciled with the words KILN FARM NAVY.

We went on excursions over the course of several summers on the river that took us to the Magic Gardens. There was one outing where there were 30 or so tubes, including a couple we had provisioned with coolers filled with beer and ice. Our navy was a formidable sight, and other tubers gave our captain's-hatted armada wide berth.

The wood stove chugged away in cold weather. But while stretches of milder temperatures in late fall and early spring were welcome, these could be dangerous times. This is because creosote would build up in the flue pipes when the stove was turned down for several days, and this tar-like substance is highly flammable. So we would have controlled burns by turning up the stove to its highest setting. The creosote would eventually catch fire with a *whoomf!* and burn off with pops and crackles. The buildup became so bad on a few occasions that the flue pipes would turn a scary red during a controlled burn because of the intense heat, and seemed to be on the verge of blowing apart.

We knew of other wood stove users who sometimes were not so fortunate during these temperature transitions, and there occasionally were destructive fires.

The Birthday Blizzard was so named because it began snowing on Dadd's birthday and didn't stop until well into my birthday, the next day. Shell, or rather the Ouija board she was tinkering with at the kitchen table, had predicted this event a couple of days earlier. So had the Weather Bureau, as well as Bix's knees, which descended into paroxysms of aches as the barometer plummeted.

My housemates and I never needed a reason to party. The storm certainly was one and we celebrated it with the kind of glee we felt as kids upon awakening on a no-school snow day. The kitchen was well lardered with coffee, beer, cognac and victuals. The porch was stacked high with firewood, Shell, Bix and everyone else had evacuated to New Park, and radio reports confirmed that the region had come to a standstill. We were toasty. The pipes hadn't frozen. The lights flickered a few times, but had not gone out, although the telephone line running along the short driveway was down. Nobody could call us and nobody could reach us. Oh joy!

Noonish, the snow stopped, the sun came out and the sky cleared into an azure blue. The kitchen was suffused with the aroma of the potpourri simmering in the kettle atop the wood stove. Dadd, Jack and I sipped coffee and nibbled on the dregs of a fruitcake sent to us by Owen Owen, our Irish friend.

Snow was blowing off the trees. A titmouse noshed on a platform feeder outside a kitchen window. And suddenly was gone as a hawk swooped down, scooped it up and flew away. How glorious it felt to be alive, even if one little bird no longer was.

I was the first person thereabouts who had a goose down jacket some decades before North Face became trendy fashion wear. I had bought the jacket on a trip to Colorado, and it made me look like the Michelin Man. But boy was it warm.

Jacketed, gloved and booted in knee-high gaiters, I clomped around the yard, a mug of coffee laced with cognac in one hand and a yardstick in the other listening to the crunch of my footfalls and the occasional caw of a crow. It otherwise was wonderfully quiet.

About 35 inches of snow had fallen. There were wind-driven drifts up to five feet high, one of which had nearly covered an Alberta blue spruce that Doctor Duck and Davis had purloined from a tree nursery on a Christmas Eve when they were feeling holiday-ish and decided the farm had to have a tree. Portions of the short driveway were impassable, while the long driveway, which was a good quarter-mile in length from the house to the state road, had disappeared, as had the cars and most of my bus.

I had just come back into the kitchen when our reverie was shattered. There was the unmistakable whine of machinery, and it was coming our way. The whine grew louder and the source revealed itself at the milk house turn to be three snow blowers operated in tandem by King Mike and a couple of pals. We stood dumbstruck at a kitchen window as they passed the house in a cloud of blown snow and continued down the long driveway.

We had visitors and the farm now had a toboggan run.

The toboggan run was fast that first afternoon, and lightning fast the second, because temperatures had come up long enough for it to rain lightly and then plunged back down, freezing the run to an icy sheen.

Within a couple of days, we had improved the run until we were able to climb onto a toboggan on a barn ramp, push off, and slowly gain speed as the toboggan sliced through the parking area adjacent to the kitchen porch and picked up serious speed on the first downhill stretch.

We had banked the hard turn down the driveway. If a toboggan made it through the turn without flipping over -- and if Jack was aboard one of the four-person rides he'd reach into his bag of nautical terms and shout "emergency full astern!" -- with everyone leaning hard to avoid being spilled, we were able to continue down the rest of the driveway and across the state road, where King Mike and his merry snow blowers had continued the course for another couple hundred feet. Traffic was very light in the days after the blizzard, but as a precaution we put a spotter on the hill where the driveway met the road with the *BEST EVER!* Flag Day party flag. The spotter would wave it if there were cars coming.

King Mike and his posse had lugged in a case of cognac and a keg of beer, which along with a goodly-sized chunk of hashish, fortified the ever flowing and ebbing crowd of tobogganers, sledders and cross-country skiers who beat a path to the farm over the next several days.

Then we discovered we were out of pot.

The five-gallon buckets we had filled the previous autumn save for one, had been buried around the farm, and finding them was impossible with nearly three feet of snow on the ground. Then Jack recalled he had buried a bucket in the earth floor of the shed. He and I repaired there, shovels in hand.

Jack paced back and forth like a pirate sizing up a beach where there was buried treasure, found a spot he liked, pushed the shovel into the floor, and then jumped on it.

The result was a happy *clink!* as it hit the lid of the bucket.

CHAPTER FIFTEEN

*"I went lickety-splitly out
to my old Fifty-Five
As I pulled away slowly, feelin' so holy,
God knows I was feelin' alive"*

   I was driving southbound toward New Park on the state road in my VW bus. About a quarter mile away came the northbound Doctor Duck in The Pig, his tricked-out Buick Special. There were no other cars on the road. We sped closer and closer to each other, and then in a feat of mind-reading legerdemain, he veered into my lane and I into his, as we shot past each other at about 50 miles an hour.

   Not exactly an everyday occurrence, but the moment is representative of our *laissez faire* attitude about driving and Kiln Farm's eclectic motor pool. In addition to my bus and The Pig, this aggregation included the Duckmobile, Hawk's vintage Chevrolet pickup truck, a Morris Minor, various GMC pickups and an

International Harvester pickup, VW Beetles, several Volvos, Big Blue, a Chevelle and Bix's Saab Stories.

The Pig was something else altogether. Doctor Duck had taken a stock late 1960s Buick Special with a slate gray body and tan vinyl roof, jacked up the rear and installed a heavy-duty suspension. Why I don't know, but as a result The Pig looked like it was a big cat about to pounce.

He bought a pair of surplus military aircraft landing lights that he bolted to the front bumper and illuminated through a second battery in the trunk. Even at the hellacious speeds he sometimes drove, The Pig never outran these lights. The *coup de grace* was a vintage eight-track tape deck he installed in the dashboard at a time when cassette players ruled and compact discs were still well over the horizon. I all too vividly recall that the only tapes he had were Neil Young's *After the Gold Rush*, KISS's *Love Gun*, The Moody Blues' *A Question of Balance*, The Box Tops' *Super Hits*, and *Dueling Banjos* from the movie *Deliverance*. All became painfully old, I have only been able to again listen to *After the Gold Rush* in the last few years, while the *Deliverance* theme music still makes me want to tear out what little hair I have.

Bix was as problematic a mechanic as he had been an Army cook, but he was a good poker player and arrived home one night in a metallic green Chevelle station wagon he had won in a game after one of the players had run out of money and bet his car. While Bix worked on many cars, he seldom got around to maintaining his own. The Chevelle's engine eventually blew up because he'd forgotten to put oil in it.

The Duckmobile was a central part of Doctor Duck's alter ego. It was a white 1960s Morris Minor so small he could barely squeeze into the driver's seat, and had to drive hunched over the steering wheel. That was the idea, as inspired by the trove of *Zap Comix* stashed in the second floor closet, some of which had cartoons with Minor-like cars passing pedestrians with weird ambulations -- both trademarks of cartoonist R. Crumb.

Doctor Duck was headed back to the farm from a Halloween party in the Duckmobile decked out in his red lamé jumpsuit with *MARS* embroidered on the back and his head and arms painted the customary red, and a bottle of Jim Beam bourbon sprayed with red sparkle paint in one hand. He spun off the road and the Duckmobile rolled down an embankment. It landed on its roof.

God does look out for fools and drunks. Doctor Duck, qualifying as both, suffered nothing worse than a small bump on his head. He climbed through a window, scrambled up the embankment and hailed a passing car.

I came down the next morning to the sight of him asleep in his jumpsuit, his head on the kitchen table. He awoke and shot me a pained look, one of the few occasions on which he dropped his carefully maintained guard. He was in desperate need of a hot soak, so I drew him a bath -- possibly the first and last bath that any of us took at the farm.

We were never able to completely scrub out the red ring he left behind.

There were perhaps a half a dozen 1955 GMC pickups at the farm at any one time, but Zarnie would have only one on the road. He scavenged the others for parts.

A few years after Zarnie moved to Colorado, a friend flatbedded all but one of the remaining GMCs to a junkyard. That pickup couldn't be removed, at least not without a chainsaw, because a box elder had grown between the front bumper and grille. This was very cool looking, so the truck was granted a reprieve. It eventually disappeared under an arbor of ivy and multiflora rose that flourished under the tree.

Hawk's excellence as a mechanic was on offer when the driveshaft of his 1937 Chevrolet pickup, which he had retrofitted with a mid-1950s straight-six Chevy engine, seized up on Marathon on one of our trips to the Florida Keys. As luck would have it, and several lifetimes of luck accrued to us, there was a junkyard across the road. In the back was, of course, a pickup with a working driveshaft of the same vintage. Hawk and Jack negotiated a price, dropped the driveshaft from the junker and swapped out the bad shaft. We were back on the road in about an hour.

Big Blue was a low-riding early 1960s blue Chevrolet Impala we bought for Pattie when she decided she wanted to be able to drive, something she had never got around to learning to do. We figured this boat of a car would be perfect for her because it was an easy-to-power steer automatic while nothing else in the farm's fleet was. Pattie was definitely not stick shift material.

She was able to do a fair approximation of driving after several lessons with Bix, who became her instructor after drawing the proverbial short straw. He was a paragon of white-knuckled patience. Eventually lessoned and licensed, Pattie would commute a mile or so to a pottery studio a couple of afternoons a week where she sanded pots to earn spending money.

She never put more than a dollar or two of gas in Big Blue, and we became accustomed to her calls to tell us she had run out of gas.

Doctor Doc's Bloody Mary red International Harvester pickup was enormous and massively dysfunctional. It seldom ran. When it did, it rattled and shook, had lousy traction going uphill in the fields, and would become stuck in reverse, hence the sight of Doc backing up a driveway, his head out the window as he shouted *"Cautio! Cautio!"* in Latin, warning chickens, ducks and other critters to get out of the way.

Rafe, Meatball and I were in California. I had left my bus with him in San Francisco while I flew down to San Diego to hang out with a guy I had known in Nam, and his wife. We spent much of my visit watching the Watergate hearings on television. More out of boredom, I think, than any sense of being a part of the great unraveling of the Nixonian assault on the Constitution, although I did think that John Dean's wife, Maureen, who sat at his side in the Senate hearing room, was hot.

I flew back to San Francisco, and Rafe met me at the airport. I got behind the wheel and motored onto the freeway connecting the airport and city. Drivers honked their horns and waved at us, some giving the V-sign they sped past.

I wondered what the heck was going on.

It was only when we arrived back in the city that I noticed Rafe had slapped a sticker on the bus's back bumper with a cartoon profile of Tricky Dick and the words:

HONK IF YOU THINK HE'S GUILTY

Among the VW Beetles was a green one driven by Bigfoot, who twice managed the feat of missing a hard left turn on the state road a mile or so from the farm, and drove through a barbed wire fence into a cow pasture.

The first time a farmer heard the crash, arrived quickly on the scene on a tractor, and towed the VW out of the field. Bigfoot had come eye to eye with a big and very surly bull. It was Bruno, the former resident of the farm. Later, when Bigfoot had another crash and an encore encounter with Bruno, the farmer claimed to have slept through the drama, eventually arriving only the next morning.

Another Beetle was actually an international orange Super Beetle, which had an extended nose and therefore more trunk space. Shell had bought it to ferry Snatchabanana around. It was a pillar of reliability even though she was a gear grinder, and Bix repeatedly had to remind her it was time to change the oil or do a tune-up.

Shell eventually looked this gift horse in the mouth and traded it for a beige early 1960s Mercedes 190D diesel sedan with a 200,000 mile pedigree. This usually would not be a problem as these classics -- ubiquitous as taxis in Europe and the Middle East -- routinely put upwards of half a million miles on the clock. Shell, however, soon discovered it would cost a couple of thousand bucks to make it roadworthy. She breathlessly told us this was her dream car, or at least the car her yogi told her she should buy.

She sold the Merc back to the mechanic she had bought it from at a loss, and ponied up for another international orange Super Beetle.

What Doc referred to as "skylarking" I called the Kiln Farm Steer. This involved staying on the road while balancing a beer, the fixings for a joint and a rolling paper. The skylarker -- and Jack and Hawk were the best -- would put a beer between his legs while holding a baggie in one hand and a rolling paper in the other, all the while steering with a knee while the joint was assembled, with pauses for quaffs of beer, reaching behind the front seats to discard empties, and reel in new beers without taking his eyes off the road.

Driving the bus with the lights off on a back road on a night when the moon was full was about as daring as I got, but Jack and Hawk were able to do The Steer while accelerating, braking and clutching, and even while turning corners no matter what the moon and weather were up to.

I felt safe when riding with Jack and Hawk, but experienced feelings bordering on terror when I got into The Pig.

We had been invited to a party down the shore, which is what people in Philadelphia say when they are going to the beach. The party was notable for all of the off-duty New York City cops getting stoned in the backyard, in all likelihood with marijuana they had confiscated. Jack, Hawk, Dad and I were pretty lit ourselves when we piled back into The Pig about 12:30 in the morning to drive to North Jersey and a bar run by friends.

Last call at this bar was 2 a.m. and it would not normally be possible to make the trip in less than an hour and a half, but Doctor Duck did it in half that time. The Pig ran full out on the Garden State Parkway, landing lights ablaze, with stops at two toll plazas, the change basket at the first receiving the last pocket change anyone had, and the second a partially eaten sub sandwich contributed by Jack.

Jack was slow to anger, but when he did boil over he was like a low pressure weather trough and not even load-bearing walls were safe from his wrath.

We were driving across a narrow two-lane viaduct at a reservoir near the farm when a dump truck began to tailgate Jack's Beetle. He tried to shake the truck, but it continued to ride his back bumper. Jack slowed to a crawl and then stopped. He got out, walked back to the truck, climbed onto the running board, reached inside past the stunned driver, pulled the key from the ignition and hurled it into the reservoir. He then drove off.

Dadd had a handsome hunter green Beetle that he bought after graduating from college. It ran beautifully for years but the interior eventually showed the effects -- and the corresponding smells -- of transporting home baby goats and pigs.

For those of us with Beetles and I my bus, our bible was *John Muir's How to Keep Your Volkswagen Alive: A Manual*

IN THE LAND

of Step-by-Step Procedures for the Complete Idiot, which predated the Idiot's Guide books by a couple of decades.

This classic shade tree mechanic tome was first published in 1969 and I vaguely recall that the oil- and grease-stained copy we shared was a spiral-bound second edition. The instructions for replacing brake shoes were typical of this quirkily written manual and read something like:

(1.) Remove the wheel hub caps, hubs and wheel.

(2.) Remove the bottom springs holding the shoes to the brakes, then the pins and the little round thing on the braking plate.

(3.) Remove the top springs in the same manner.

(4.) Open and drink a beer.

(5.) Now you can put on the new shoes.

And so on and so forth.

How to Keep Your Volkswagen Alive is now in its 19th edition.

Doctor Duck eventually graduated to Volvos and sold Dan the baby blue station wagon in which Pattie and little Caitlin perished. His own everyday car was a faded red four-door Volvo sedan. He bought a decal at the bookstore of a state college not far from the farm where he was going through the motions of taking a chemistry course, painstakingly rearranged some of the letters, and affixed them to the rear window. They read:

UNIVERSITY OF THE STREET

Dadd then caught the Volvo bug. He and Doctor Duck bought several parts cars that were parked in various states of disassembly around the shed. His everyday car was a navy blue station wagon in terrific condition, that is until he loaned it to Callie to drive to work at a restaurant where she was a bartender.

Callie had a peripheral vision problem in her right eye and succeeded in skeeving the right side body work of Dadd's beautiful wagon from front to back after driving too close to a wall. She then did the same thing to a white station wagon Dadd had rebuilt and loaned her, but the *coup de grâce* was applied early on a brutally cold Christmas morning when she ran the wagon up onto a traffic island hidden under drifting snow after over serving herself at last call.

All four tires came off their wheels, a problem that under normal circumstances would have been impossible to remedy in the middle of the night, let alone a holiday, but because there was a goodly pile of tires on wheels from all the parts cars, the problem was remedied fairly easily, if painfully, by Dadd and I. We fortified ourselves against the snowy, near-zero conditions between tire changes by retiring to a warm car and taking chugs from a thermos of coffee liberally spiked with cognac. The first glimmer of sunrise was appearing on the horizon by the time we had finished, well in our cups. Callie, meanwhile, had sobered up.

VW bus engines seldom made it beyond 150,000 miles even with regular oil changes and other maintenance, and mine packed in at almost precisely that milestone.

This would have seriously cramped my style, especially going to the New Park Tavern. But Dadd and Doctor Duck had a Volvo parts car, a pumpkin orange sedan with a single working headlight and taillight that wasn't registered and had no tags, so it couldn't be driven legally. *This* problem was solved by taking a slow and tortuous route to New Park on largely disused dirt roads pocked with deep potholes and washouts paralleling the creek past David's Rock that deposited me at the edge of New Park, where I could leave the Volvo in a woods and hoof it the last quarter mile or so to the tavern. What was normally a 15-minute drive each way became a gut wrenching, head banging odyssey, the high grass between the rut marks brushing against the underside of the car like ocean waves, that took about an hour and made considerably worse because the Volvo's suspension was shot. I was quite happy when my engine had been rebuilt and I was back on real road.

Bix was attracted to a succession of women whose cars he would work on. One day he worked on the Saab Story of his latest crush. Job completed, he repaired to the kitchen sink to wash his hands.

"I thought you were going to drive So and So's car back into town when you were finished," Jack remarked much too matter of factly. Something was up.

"I am," Bix replied. "Why do you ask?"

"Well, then why is her car going backwards down the driveway?"

We ran from the house to see the Saab Story bump down the long driveway, gradually picking up speed until it ran up a bank at the curve, dinged the huge sycamore, and flipped over. Bix had forgotten to set the hand brake.

CHAPTER SIXTEEN

*"Gone are the days we stopped to decide
Where we should go
We just ride"*

It had dawned on me while flying home from Nam that I knew more about the Far East than East Los Angeles. So while most of my friends -- the sensible ones, anyway -- were getting married, buying houses and raising families in the 1970s, I was seeing the U S of A in my VW bus when not hanging at Kiln Farm.

I bought the bus new for $3,100 in cash, pretty much what remained of the money that I had sent home from the war. It was a stripped-down white Kombi model with nothing between the two-seat front cabin and a 1.7 liter boxer engine in the rear except a stamped steel floor. The engine made an underwhelming 67 horsepower.

The bus had a four-speed manual transmission. Once I got the hang of shifting to take advantage of what momentum there was, and momentum was the name of the game with a brick-like VW bus. I could keep up with most traffic on interstates and crawl to the top of the highest mountain passes while praying that the air-cooled engine would not blow up in the thin air. (Which, as noted, it eventually did.)

I customized the Kombi by bolting on oversized truck side-view mirrors, building a carpeted floor between the front and engine with compartments underneath where we stashed coolers, sleeping bags and such. This left the upper floor pretty much clear. Kind of like the hideaway qualities of a room in a traditional Japanese house, or so I imagined.

Next, I installed an aerodynamically sleek Plexiglas bubble dome on the roof. This had been fabricated by a guy who lived near Woodstock, New York. I'd seen his ad in *The Whole Earth Catalog*, a counterculture catalog devoted to sustainable living. I was concerned that the pitch of the dome would not perfectly match that of the roof, but the template I drew for him with Doctor Doc's help was precise and the dome fit snugly after we cut a hole in the roof with a sawzall, applied latex bathtub caulking and ratcheted down eight stainless steel carriage bolts. The dome never leaked and light would pour into the bus even when the floral design side and rear curtains and a curtain between the front seats and Japanese room were drawn. I used a swatch of leftover

IN THE LAND

curtain material to cover the jacket of the journal I was writing in at the time.

When it came to our road trips in the bus, the farm was like the hub of a giant if lopsided wheel, the most frequent destinations being Zarnie's places in Colorado in the summer and the Florida Keys in the winter.

Ours --my housemates and I -- was the last generation to know the United States in the plural. Beyond Colorado and the Keys, we embarked on an on-again, off-again exploration of 46 of the contiguous 48 states minus Kentucky and Montana for no particular reason. Crossing a state line -- let alone the Continental Divide, which I probably did 30 or so times during the decade -- was a big deal, as was taking an exit ramp off an interstate before exit ramps everywhere led to the same fast-food joints, convenience stores and gas stations incapable of making even the most rudimentary repairs no matter where you were.

I had loved looking at maps since I was a boy; a reproduction of a 16th century Mercator cylindrical projection map of the world hung on a wall across from my bed, and I studied it endlessly. After a few years, the door pockets of the my bus bulged with maps collected on our travels, but I seldom consulted them.

Getting lost was no big deal, and it was an adventure to follow the thin blue line representing a routeless and nameless out-of-the-way road in the *Rand McNally Travel Atlas*.

I have so many memories of being on the road in the bus, and came to see my travels in koan-like terms: The journey *was* the reward.

Waking at dawn's early light at the edge of a pasture off Interstate 80 near Rock Springs, Wyoming and drowsily realizing that Jack and I were being watched. I slowly turned in my sleeping bag and opened one eye to be greeted by the sight of 10 or so curious horses and a lone cow who had apparently been adopted by the horses. Only a single strand of barbed wire fence separated us.

When I unzipped my bag, stood up and stretched, the horses and cow backed off a few feet but then stopped. They watched me do my ablutions, which included emptying my bladder, washing my face and hands in a water bucket and brushing my teeth. I suppose they didn't have much company out in the middle of nowhere because they seemed disappointed when we motored off after drinking coffee and eating breakfast heated on a camp stove.

Sitting out a downpour in the Florida Everglades so torrential and long lasting that the bus began to feel like a Turkish bath. Our confinement was not without entertainment as we watched a hawk alight on a fence post in ferocious winds, get blown off and then embarrassedly flap back up onto its roost.

Binoculars in hand, watching a magnificent and at that time exceedingly rare condor land in the highest branches of a towering Ponderosa pine near Santa Clarita in Southern California. I became spaced out in the heat later the same day and left my wallet with a goodly amount of traveler's checks atop a soda vending machine at a gas station off Interstate 5 near Coalinga in Central California, drove 100 or so miles toward our destination in Oregon before realizing what had happened, and backtracked. The wallet was still there.

Standing on a corner in Winslow, Arizona. A flatbed Ford pickup truck passed by with music blaring. It was Jackson Browne singing the lyrics "I'm standing on a corner in Winslow, Arizona, and such a fine sight to see, a flatbed Ford . . . "

Seeing the sun-draped vistas of Oakland and San Francisco emerge on a July morning as Seals & Croft's "Summer Breeze" came on the radio.

Sitting at a traffic light where Columbus Avenue bisects Broadway in San Francisco's North Beach neighborhood. Jane was driving and I was reading *The Dharma Bums*, a semi-fictional book set in California and based on Jack Kerouac's experiences with Buddhism. Ray Smith, the Kerouac character, was walking across the very intersection in the book as we waited for the light to turn green.

Driving around a bend on a mountain road in Colorado and coming upon a herd of cattle being driven to their summer range by cowboys on horses, as well as a cowboy driving the first all-terrain vehicle any of us had seen. The road had numerous switchbacks, and twice more the herd and cowboys crossed our path as we made our way to the top of the mountain and a pass that still had a goodly amount of by-then filthy black snow although it was August.

Having the driver's side mirror sheared off by a low flying crow on a long downhill run on Interstate 84 near the Idaho-Oregon state line, braking to a stop and

IN THE LAND

walking uphill where the only traces of the bird were scattered feathers. We didn't find the mirror.

   Developing engine trouble near Nashville, Tennessee and coasting off the highway, through an interchange and straight into the parking lot of an auto parts store where I was able to swap out a fouled spark plug and we soon were on the road again.

   Coming upon "Falling Rock" signs on Interstate 80 westbound near Truckee, California on a scorching summer day as the dust was settling around a boulder about the size of my bus that had separated from a towering rock face and crashed into the roadway. While pondering what to do, I recalled a geologist friend of Zarnie's who also drove a VW bus, his with a bumper sticker that read

GEOLOGISTS KNOW THEIR SCHIST

and liked to remark that "Falling Rock" signs are always good news for folks in his line of work. I, however, summoned a vision of a day squandered as we waited hours for a crane to arrive and remove the bolder and as the ice melted in our coolers. Jack, Hawk, Jane and I had to binge eat to keep the food from spoiling. Valor being the better part of discretion, we crept between the boulder and rock face with Jack directing me with the kind of hand signals a landing officer would use on an aircraft carrier flight deck. The bus made it with a couple of inches to spare.

Pausing for lunch at a pullout at Donner Pass near Lake Tahoe on the eastbound return trip -- which was considerably easier in the bus because the western slope was less steep than the eastern -- and realizing mid-bite that this was where a pioneer wagon train was forced to spend a winter in the late 1840s because of impassably deep snow. Fewer than half of these emigrants survived and some had to resort to cannibalism. My sandwich suddenly didn't taste so good.

Driving into a dusty South Dakota hamlet, the name of which I have long forgotten, with Shell and Jack. It had an unpaved main street and but a single business was open, a cafe with a sign in the window reading "The Home of Apple Pie a la Mode" minus the accent mark over the "a." There was a display case filled with dinosaur bones behind the lunch counter that the waitress explained the owner had prospected for in North Dakota. We, of course, ordered the house specialty. The check, with coffee and refills, came to two bucks and change. We left her a five-dollar bill.

Roaming among the maze of buttes and spires in the South Dakota Badlands later in the day with heads full of magic mushrooms. In my torpor, I was imagining that the land on which we trod had not felt a footfall in a millennium, a silly thought that dissipated as I realized we had become disoriented and were lost as a ferocious thunderstorm blew in. Wetter, if not wiser, we eventually found our way out.

Setting out from the farm on a Colorado-bound trip just as the sun, partially obscured by scudding clouds, began to drop beneath the horizon. If I squinted a little the clouds looked like an archipelago of islands in an inland sea, their tops resembling torn cotton and the underbellies vibrant salmon pink, cinnabar orange and goldenrod yellow hues. They were offset by two bright evening stars -- Venus and Saturn, actually. The scene could have been painted by Maxfield Parrish, with musical accompaniment by Pink Floyd.

Going on a slow-motion, dawn-to-dusk trip down a rutted dirt road -- one of those thin blue lines in the *Rand McNally* -- from Wyoming into northwestern Colorado. There were oil and gas drilling rigs, but we saw no sign of human habitation for the entire 80-mile trip save for the occasional mailbox at the foot of a road to an unseen ranch. There is a time of day in climes like this that I cherish: The light is still high on the ridge tops but darkness has descended in the valleys. One this day there was a bonus -- a sunset that was an encore of the Parrish-Floyd spectacular, although without the planets.

    Picking up a hitchhiking teenager and his Border Collie on Interstate 80 in State Line, Nevada while traveling with Rafe and Meatball. The kid revealed a couple of hundred miles later than he was running away from home. We stopped for gas at Winnemucca and told him to call home on my dime. He did and we arranged for he and his dog to be picked up by his mother at the local sheriff's office.

    Being propositioned by a lady toll collector on Interstate 70 near Lawrence, Kansas. I told her that I was flattered. Jack and Jane tittered from the back of the bus as I pulled away.

    Hiking the Bright Angel Trail from the South Rim of the Grand Canyon in new hiking boots that I had not bothered to break in.

This sin did not make its presence felt until a mile or so into the 12-mile ascent, which was an excruciating embarrassment as a group of elderly women passed me at one point. Jane suggested I rent a mule for the rest of the climb, but I was too proud to do such a sensible thing. My feet were a bloody mess by the time we made it to the top and I had to wear flip-flops for several weeks while they healed.

Taking a side road off Interstate 15 in Nevada on a whim and unexpectedly coming upon a ghost town whose name we were unable to ascertain. The only sign was one warning

The Fire Danger
Today Is
EXTREME

which must have been the case for many years. There was a 1940s vintage Reo truck with a stake body parked behind a one-time general store that looked as if it was ready to roll with gas and a battery. Stuff just didn't rust in that environment.

Exploring the vestiges of the Anasazi Pueblo civilization with Shell, Hawk and Jack that had suddenly and inexplicably vanished in the 14th century from the Four Corners region where Colorado, Utah, New Mexico and Arizona come together.

Zarnie led us to an outcropping under which was a cave covered with petroglyphs he said were a well kept secret. The wall carvings were extraordinary. The discarded pizza boxes, beer cans and condoms were not. After the sun set, we laid on the still warm ground taking in the vast, star-filled sky, the Milky Way running from horizon to horizon like a celestial river. Even if I was perfectly still and focused on one patch of sky, this astral show didn't seem to be moving. How could that be? It of course was moving, which eventually was confirmed when I focused on the sky immediately above the "chest" of the recumbent Indian on Sleeping Ute Mesa. New stars trickled into view every few minutes.

Camping a few hundred miles away in southern Arizona a day later with the same crew, awakening just before dawn to watch the brilliant orange flowers of the Saguaro cactus open for a precious few minutes and then slowly close as the sun broke above the horizon. We later drove down State Route 85 to the unusually named hamlet of Why on the Mexican border. In a-tisket-a-tasket unison, we stepped into Mexico and then back into the U.S. several times.

Seeing a lightning strike raise an enormous cloud of sand as we crossed the Bonneville Salt Flats in Utah.

Being waved off Interstate 10 west of Yuma, Arizona by a California Highway Patrol officer because of dangerously high desert winds that had toppled a Camel Express ("We're Humping To Serve You Better") tractor and tandem trailers, which lay forlornly on their backs, their wheels facing skyward like a herd of dead elephants.

Shell, Hawk and I spent that evening at a roadhouse with a bar into which hundreds of silver dollars had been imbedded. There was a jukebox full of honky-tonk 45s and we took turns buying rounds of beers, feeding the jukebox, swapping stories and dancing with a delightful group of strangers while the children of one couple played Hackysack in a corner.

CHAPTER SEVENTEEN

"Get outta Denver better go, go
Get outta Denver better go-ooooh"

It was Colorado's incredible natural diversity, as well as my friendship with Zarnie, that drew me back so many times. In the course of a two-hour drive, you could go from Ponderosa pine forests, to tablelands chockablock with mesas, to high desert, to alpine foothills and 14,000-foot mountains.

Zarnie was a high school valedictorian who graduated from the demanding chemical engineering program at the university in New Park. He also played national championship-caliber football. He was and remains certifiably crazy. As in knocking out every streetlamp on the university mall from a one-time girlfriend's dormitory at the south end to his fraternity house on the north end. Because he was a jock, he only got a wrist slap. More recently, he cross-country skied off a cliff and landed in a ravine. He was fine other than a few cracked ribs and head-to-toe bruises.

He landed a well-paying job with a Fortune 500 chemical company right out of college. But as someone who always looked like he had just come in from a long hike, he wasn't cut out for a confining, artificially lit life of neckties, lab coats and pocket protectors. Zarnie quit after a few months and alighted at Kiln Farm. That also was too confining, and he eventually headed out West for the autonomy so many people had sought before him.

The Roaring Fork River starts near Aspen and runs undisturbed, which is to say undammed, to its confluence with the Colorado River some 70 miles northwest near Glenwood Springs. It is a river of many personalities as it wanders through meanders created over the millennia. At its source above Aspen's tony vacation homes, it is a rivulet. At its terminus near the Glenwood cemetery where "Doc" Holliday of Gunfight at OK Corral fame is buried, it is fairly wide, comparatively docile and navigable by raft and shallow draft boat.

Carbondale is more or less at the halfway point and it was on a ranch just outside town -- Easterners like myself would call it a farm -- that Zarnie eventually settled. Jack, Hawk and Eldon were to follow, as eventually did Shell, who finally lassoed Hawk after years of trying.

  Shell called the guys the Slow Children, so named because of the

SLOW
CHILDREN

sign on the highway below the house.

  This was the time when, as the joke went, Carbondale was first attracting the attention of the millionaires who were being driven out of Aspen by the billionaires. In any event, we were treated like royalty on our visits and weren't allowed to pay for a coffee at the Village Smithy or a beer at the Hollywood Saloon -- Easterners would call it a bar -- because we were from a farm back East that had taken on mythical proportions. The Slow Children were much loved and beyond their antics gave back mightily to the tight-knit community. This included a project supervised by Hawk to pave Carbondale's main street for the first time. As one local put it, the Slow Children wore out bar stools but never their welcome.

  The Hollywood had a sort of louche glory about it and was straight out of a Western movie with swinging saloon doors, a high stamped tin ceiling, immense mirrored bar back, a few tables and a brass spittoon. All the place seemed to lack was a piano with a guy in a boater and striped shirt with arm garters banging out tunes between knocking back beers, although there was a jukebox and television.

  Back at the farm, Jack, Hawk and Eldon pitched in to buy a 1950s era International Harvester school bus that had once transported handicapped kids. They painted the bus a hunter's camouflage mélange of browns and tans and converted it into a camper with bunk beds, seats, a table and kitchenette. It was christened Zytax Zymo. Zytax was a made-up word and Zymo short for zymology, the science of fermentation. As Hawk put it, "We plan to ferment all over the country." And so they did.

  A male and female Muscovy duck were culled from the farm flock, given the names Fucky and Lucky in the expectation that they would breed at the Slow Children House, crated and loaded onto the Zymo for a grand send-off that was supposed to be on a Friday morning, but happily extended on through a Memorial Day weekend to a belated and semi-tearful Tuesday departure. I still have a photograph I took just before their departure: Jack, Hawk, Pattie and Eldon are soft-shoeing chorus line style in front of the Zymo, their right legs kicking out in a semblance of syncopation.

Several of us showed up at the Slow Children House later in the year. There were already a couple of dozen Fucky and Lucky offspring head bopping and *heh-heh* hissing around the place as Muscovys do in their slapstick way. The Zymo had been converted again, this time into a lumber storage shed, and later made its last trip to the banks of the Roaring Fork where Hawk built a studio in it for a potter friend.

The Slow Children House was a crazy quilt of period building styles.

The oldest part, which locals said dated to the late 19th century, included the kitchen. Its walls were made of logs chinked with slaked lime, wood shavings and cow manure. There still were some original shot glass panes in the windows and a board nailed to a wall with the faded names and heights of the children of the pioneers who first lived there as they grew.

The middle part, built of pinkish-red brick by the Civilian Conservation Corps during the Great Depression, included the living and dining rooms. The knotty pine walls were insulated with balled-up copies of the *Denver Post*, judging from a board that had come loose.

The newest part -- containing two bedrooms and a bath -- was constructed of post-World War II manufactured plank siding with jalousie windows. It was ugly by comparison. A fairly new corrugated tin roof covered the entire house.

The house had come with a cross-eyed gray tabby cat with a broken tail and an overarching insolence, hence a sign next to the kitchen door that read

Don't Let The Damned Cat In

and a magpie by the name of Mike who was named for a guy named Mike who talked like a magpie. The feathered Mike would sit on a split-rail fence behind the house flapping his wings and mimicking the cat and Muscovys when not going *quardle oodle ardle wardle doodle*, a call I painstakingly phoneticized in my journal.

While the grass in the one-time pastureland beyond the house was burned yellow because of a lack of rainfall, the yard was a rich golf course green. This was because Zarnie had mastered the art of negotiating water rights -- which in an arid place like Colorado are more important than any other kind of rights, including that inalienable American right to bear arms. The result was that he had diverted water from a creek on a neighboring ranch down a series of narrow channels he had dug and through sluices he had built at intervals. The water ran at a trickle, but a trickle was all the Slow Children needed over the long haul to meet their needs.

The irrigation scheme resulted in a rude awakening one morning as I lay sleeping in my tent in the yard. The Muscovys woke me with a frenzy of hissing and splashing. Zarnie had forgotten to close a sluice and water had coursed into the yard, lifting the tent and me inside it.

Water rights aside, Zarnie believed rivers were the ultimate metaphors of our existence. He opposed the unceasing efforts of the federal Bureau of Reclamation to tame the Colorado River in the Grand Canyon and other wild rivers of the West by damming them, sometimes for dubious purposes.

To Zarnie, dams were not unlike DDT, an outlawed pesticide that destroyed wildlife, especially birds. He came to understand the damage many dams had done and future dams could do. This damage included the inevitable influx of people who, after construction of dams and the immense reservoirs behind them, flocked by the hundreds of thousands into what had been fragile wildernesses that had become recreation areas with the big city noise, litter, pollution and crime they had sought to leave behind.

   The record of opposition to dams in Colorado and throughout the West has been decidedly mixed. Conservationists prevailed in opposing a plan to dam and flood an historic valley near Zarnie's eventual home that had originally been settled by Native Americans and later by whites, but lost a round when another valley 50 miles away was dammed.

   When Zarnie stopped over at the farm on a trip East, he took apart the earthen and rock dam he had built on the creek below the cornfield across from the front porch, allowing the creek to once again flow freely. A few miles away, environmentalists were in the early stages of opposing an effort to dam the creek that flowed past David's Rock by the chemical company that Zarnie had briefly worked for, in service of a reservoir that would supply water for a proposed textile fiber plant. The reservoir would have flooded several thousand acres containing endangered flora and fauna, as well as historic homes, some dating back to the late 17th century. It took nearly a decade, but the good guys eventually prevailed.

The Roaring Fork Valley was a cultural backwater, and aside from the occasional pickup band at the Hollywood and a summer arts and crafts festival at Carbondale's meager municipal park, you were left to your own devices if paying big bucks to rub shoulders with the elite at an event down valley in Aspen was beyond your means, or merely a turnoff. So it was a big deal when the Jerry Garcia Band was booked into a faded vaudeville theater up valley in Glenwood Springs. It was an evening less memorable for the music, which was quite fine, than a close encounter in the men's room.

During an intermission, Jack and I were standing a few feet apart doing our business at a trough urinal when Garcia himself approached, unzipped and began doing his business. Jack, who typically was left under-awed by fame, was gobsmacked.

"N . . . ni . . . nice show," he spluttered with atypical shyness.

"Thanks," Garcia replied in his squeaky voice.

The ensuing silence was broken by a splattering sound. Jack had peed on his prized rattlesnake skin cowboy boots.

A circle of a sort was mind-blowingly closed one day when Zarnie and I drove into Montrose in southwestern Colorado at high noon. It was 120 degrees F. according to an electronic sign outside a bank.

As we headed north out of town on our way back to Carbondale, Zarnie mentioned that he knew of a place a mile or two away where we could cool off. He soon pointed to a barely noticeable opening in the cottonwood trees lining the road. I turned in and we drove about a quarter mile on an unpaved road through choking dust, parked and walked a short distance. An exquisite waterfall appeared. It was tucked into a small canyon with a few cottonwood trees and a reliquary with the statue of the Virgin Mary. There were fresh cut flowers at her feet.

I had pictured this place precisely in a dream years earlier.

CHAPTER EIGHTEEN

*"It's the Colorado Rocky Mountain High,
I've seen it raining fire in the sky.
Friends around the camp fire and everybody's high"*

Having done poorly not once but twice in geology, my science elective in college, I thought I owed it to myself, as well as my long-suffering parents, to bone up on the geology of the Rocky Mountains before my initial foray there.

This is what I found:

The Rockies were formed from 55 million to 80 million years ago during the Late Cretaceous era by something called the Laramide Orogeny, a period of intense mountain building in western North America. These mountains are adolescents compared to the Appalachians on the East Coast, which date back 480 million or so years.

The Appalachians were formed as a consequence of repeated collisions between what became North America and Europe and Africa. Such continent kissing can be ruled out for the Rockies. As can plate tectonics, the large scale motions of the Earth's outer crust, because the plates closest to the Rockies are a thousand miles away. Despite a century of research by the best geological minds, no one knows why the formation of the Rocky Mountains began and ended. I once observed Zarnie's geologist friend and an equally punctilious colleague nearly come to blows at the Hollywood over this puzzler. If ever two people needed to get a life, they were them.

What is certain is that the orogeny occurred in a series of spurts, with periods of relative quiet in between, and by the time the last spurt had spurted, there had been considerable mountain building from Canada to Mexico, including the Laramie Mountains of Wyoming for which the orogeny is named. Since then erosion by water and glaciers have sculpted the mountain range into dramatic valleys such as the Roaring Fork and peaks such as the Colorado Fourteeners, 14 peaks with elevations of 14,000 feet or more. Humans came on the scene about 18,000 years ago, toward the end of the last Ice Age, which is the blink of an eye in geological time.

While like the geologists we also did not come to blows, I had a heated discussion with a Vietnam veteran, a former Green Beret actually, one boozy evening at the Hollywood.

In an effort to understand the war, I had been trying to intellectualize it. This entailed coming to terms with the vast, untranslatable differences between the Vietnamese and American people. As journalist Frances FitzGerald wrote in *Fire in the Lake*, which I had finished reading a few days earlier, the Confucian-based history of the Vietnamese is focused on the past through the small tradition of the family and the great tradition of the state, while American history is canted toward the future, which is to say change and conquest. This, I earnestly sought to explain to the vet over a fourth or fifth Lone Star beer, was at the root of why the Vietnamese never fathomed what we were about and we them, as well as why the war was unwinnable for us politically and socially, let alone militarily.

"Bullshit. Complete, absolute and utter bullshit," the vet growled as he gathered up his beer-soaked money, leaned over and fumbled under the table. He came up with a crutch with which I briefly thought he was going to take a swing at me. He instead pushed away his chair and struggled to his feet, or I should say foot. This was because he had come home from the war with only one leg, a devastating loss that on sober reflection, my trite intellectualizing and lazy habit of being overly influenced by the last book I had read did not begin to explain.

At 12,965 feet, the twin peaks of Mt. Sopris were a dramatic backdrop to the Slow Children House, and while Sopris may not be the kind of mountain a beginner would dare to take on, it is not particularly challenging to climb.

Sturdy boots and a walking stick are about all you need. There are wire handholds the last few hundred feet to the summit of the East Peak for the light of heart and light of head, since the air at that altitude is quite thin. While glacial scree slows the ascent, it considerably speeds up the descent. If you don't mind stopping and cleaning rock shards out of your boots every few minutes, you can take the Scree Express, and an ascent that takes about 10 hours can be cut to a third of that on the way back down.

Zarnie, Jack and I set out to climb Sopris one August day with Putney, a long-haired black Labrador cross whom Zarnie had named after the title character in the movie *Putney Swope*, a 1969 cult classic. We carried enough grub in backpacks for a couple of days, while Putney had his own supply of kibble in doggy saddlebags.

  I parked my bus behind a barn at an abandoned farm just below Sopris's tree line and we filled our water bottles from a pond bordered with watercress. I wondered whether these plants were descendants of those left by a geologist whom I had read about when I boned up for the trip. He was also a medical doctor who dropped the leafy vegetable into lakes, streams and springs throughout the Rockies in a noble effort to prevent scurvy in the pioneers who stopped there to water their animals.

  We hiked to about 9,000 feet and camped for the night amidst cow pies. These were left by free ranging cows that graze the pastureland, such as it is, at higher altitudes when the weather is mild. There was also what Zarnie identified as coyote tracks, some an amazing six inches in length and most spaced close together, which he said indicated lopers who were in no particular hurry to get anywhere. We built a fire of dried cow pies, ate a leisurely meal, shared a pot of cowboy coffee and later smoked some of Jack's hashish from a small brass pipe while watching tendrils of smoke from the fire spiral into the gloaming while listening to coyote cries sounding, to my ears, like doleful bugle notes.

We rose early, undertook the final 4,000-foot leg before it became too hot, and paused at about 11,000 feet, where we watered. The sun was so bright and the wind was blowing so hard that it had a percussive quality, and my eyes kept tearing up. I regretted having left my Ray-Ban Aviators in the bus; Zarnie and Jack had been wiser. We watched a hawk careering in the thermals below us. It didn't flap its wings once.

We reached the peak in late morning. There was a visitor's registration book in a lidded wooden stand maintained by the Department of the Interior, and it appeared that "Peter Frampton," or more likely some wag who had appropriated the name of the then popular Brit rocker, was the last person to sign it.

We shed our packs and took in the view. I had climbed the not-quite-as-tall Mt. Fuji while on R&R in Japan. The view from that hallowed peak could have been beautiful, but it was spoiled by emissions from smog-covered factories probably making stuff to export to the U.S.

Sopris was none of that and much more.

Almost everywhere below us were aspens, ponderosas and limber pines. To the east was the rest of the Elk

Range, of which Sopris is a part. To the south was the lower Roaring Fork Valley and Carbondale and Aspen, which from our vantage point were obscured, although we did see a small plane begin its approach to the Aspen airport before disappearing behind a peak. To the west was Rock Glacier with its amphitheater shape and splotches of green vegetation. To the north was the upper Roaring Fork Valley and mountains that stretched to Wyoming and beyond. Four thousand miles beyond to the northernmost reach of the Rockies in Alaska, which I had seen through the window of the Freedom Bird bringing me home from the war.

Jack loaded and lit his hash pipe. He took a toke and passed the pipe to Zarnie, who also took a toke. Then it was my turn. I toked and passed out.

We had many experiences with the Slow Children House as our base, including the Rope Bridge Adventure.

Our destination that day was the aspen forest above Carbondale where the Roaring Fork more than lives up to its name as it shoots through a basalt and limestone canyon. It was sunny and quite hot, and being late summer, the meadows we crossed as we climbed to the canyon were rich with columbine, primrose, lavender and sage. I reflexively reached down to my left as we walked around a patch of lavender and ran its flower spikes through my fingers and then reached down to my right and did the same with the sage. I alternately brought the fingers on my left and right hand to my nose and breathed in the intoxicating bouquet.

While our hike was not difficult, neither was it for the faint of heart, because there was only one way to cross the canyon for several miles in either direction -- a crude wood and rope footbridge straight out of an Indiana Jones movie that screamed *DANGER!* Some of the wooden slats were missing, providing a vertiginous view of the Roaring Fork hurtling through the canyon 100 or so feet below, while the ropes holding the bridge together were not in very good shape, either.

One of the Slow Children was two or three steps onto the bridge when I sensed Shell was no longer with us. When I turned around, I saw she had stopped dead in her tracks. There was a "You've gotta be nuts" look on her face that I had seen on other occasions when she sensed, usually correctly, that sanity -- along with Elvis – had left the building.

Indiana Jones and the Temple of Doom did not premiere until a few years later, but the first time I heard this snippet of dialog between Indy (Harrison Ford) and Willie (Kate Capshaw) from that movie I knew it fit the moment perfectly:

INDY: Anything can happen. It's a long way to Delhi.

WILLIE: No, thanks, no more adventures with you, Dr. Jones.

INDY: Sweetheart, after all the fun we've had together?

WILLIE: If you think I'm going to Delhi with you, or anyplace else after all the trouble you've gotten me into, think again, buster! I'm going home to Missouri where they never feed you snakes before ripping your heart out and lowering you into hot pits. This is not my idea of a swell time.

We backtracked into the shade of an aspen grove, where a canteen and orange slices were passed around. A magpie, certainly not Mike, squawked off in the distance, but other than the thrum of the Roaring Fork coursing through the canyon, it was quiet.

Jack finally broke the silence.

"So what if I carry Shell across?" he offered. "She can close her eyes," he said as he made binoculars with his hands and scanned the horizon as if looking for a rescue ship.

Fire leaped from Shell's eyes.

More silence.

"Well, we could always throw the Ching . . . ," I suggested without much conviction.

The fire had gone out and there were now only wisps of smoke framing the what-now look on her face.

" . . . Or we could just backtrack," I added unhelpfully. "No big deal."

"Screw all of you," Shell replied. It was perhaps the only time I heard her use even mild profanity.

"I'm going to do it," she added with an unchallengeable finality. "I know how to fly this plane. It's just that I'm not always sure about landing it."

Then the most amazing but Shell-like thing happened. She was suddenly on the other side of the bridge, waving her sun hat at us.

"Come on you Slow Children!" she laughed. "What's taking you so long?"

CHAPTER NINETEEN

"It got down to sixty at the mornin' tide
Caught a three-pound grouper from the bridge
I ain't hurtin' nobody and I wouldn't hurt me
I guess I'd lie about it if I did"

If there was such a thing as a winter home for the Kiln Farm crew, it was at an enchanted place called Africa.

Africa was on Sugarloaf Key, which is situated between Park Key and Saddlebunch Keys about 20 miles from Key West. Sugarloaf is the second largest key and forms a loop on the Atlantic Ocean side, as opposed to the Gulf of Florida side, that creates the illusion of being separate islands. While this is not true, locals refer to the upper part of the key as Upper Sugarloaf and the lower part Lower Sugarloaf, and it was on Lower Sugarloaf that we found a little piece of paradise on a trip ostensibly about finally being able to catch up with Comet Kahoutek.

U.S. Route 1, the so-called Ocean Highway, runs down the spine of Sugarloaf and bisects many of the other keys, as well, most of them too small for side roads. On

Sugarloaf, however, there is an all but forgotten side road once designated Florida State Road 4A, according to rusted road signs, that begins at Bow Channel and snakes along the lower edge of the key in a lazy U-shape before rejoining Route 1 about three miles on. There are but two houses on the road, as well as the ruins of a bat tower, the relic of a failed experiment in the late 1920s to lure bats who would eat the mosquitoes that bedeviled fishermen and tourists, and continue to do so today.

We came upon an illegal dump on the landward side of the road about a mile from Bow Channel. Although you won't see photographs of these dumps in glossy tourist brochures, they are ubiquitous in the Keys. You can't dig into the rock-hard coral to bury or landfill, and many a refrigerator and automobile ends up rusting away in illegal dumps because of the expense of trucking the stuff to the mainland.

I don't recall why we decided to climb around this particular dump. Intuition, I suppose. To our delight, we found interlocking lagoons and a larger body of water of a sublime tropical blue and ringed by mangroves. There was an expanse that was part woods and part mangrove hammock hard by the lagoons that seemed to be just about perfect for camping.

The predominant tree was black mangrove, the tallest of which grew to be barely 20 feet high. There was also red mangrove, gumbo limbo, coco plum, sea grape, strangler fig and poisonwood, which as the name implies, produces a sap that can cause skin and other irritations and gives off a toxic smoke if you are stupid enough to burn it, as some campers are wont to do because the wood is accessible, soft and therefore easily cut. There also were teeming colonies of reflex air plants, members of the bromeliad family, that grew on the limbs of larger trees and sustained themselves on moisture from the night air. We would bring back a few young plants each year and attach them to a curtain rod in the window of the farmhouse bathroom where they would thrive on the southern exposure and moisture from the shower.

The fauna included several species of heron and egret, red-bellied woodpeckers, common sandpipers, mourning doves and the occasional purple gallinule and double-crested cormorant.

Green anoles are diminutive arborial lizards. They are fearless and seemed to be everywhere, including in our sleeping bags if we didn't shake them out before retiring. They would let us pick them up with our index fingers. There were several kinds of butterflies, as well as chiggers, scorpions, fire ants and mangrove spiders, a huge and hairy -- and harmless -- arthropod. And of course mosquitoes.

The lagoon where we swam and snorkeled was a wonderland of sergeant major fish, tetras, squid, octopus and barracuda, which were merely curious as we paddled about and not the least bit ferocious despite their fearsome choppers. We gave the barracuda plenty of room, especially if they were chaperoning youngsters, and they did the same.

Africa's only drawback was the lack of running water. This problem was kind of solved by showering at Lazy Lakes Campground at the Bow Channel Bridge, which was run by a kindly left-handed Mormon by the name of Veryl. One morning Veryl called Jack and me into his office. We expected to be told -- in gentle terms, because Veryl seemed incapable of being angry -- that we had worn out our welcome, even if we did buy several bags of ice and other odds and ends each day from he and his wife. Instead he declared he had noticed we both were southpaws and presented us with membership cards in the Lazy Lakes Left-Handed Club.

Mine read:

Shaun Mullen, having been proven of sound mind, good fellowship and fidelity to the Brotherhood, is hereby designated a member of the Lazy Lakes Left-Handed Club, meriting full honors and prerogatives. With all rights and privileges afforded by the Government to members of minority groups. No more to be the brunt of lefthanded jokes. Henceforth all monkey wrenches, moustache cups, scissors, can-openers, nuts, bolts and loose screws, etc., must be equally made for Lazy Lakes Left-Handed Club.

We didn't linger long in the Keys on our inaugural visit. Comet Kahoutek had been a bust. And as someone who had grown up and lived amidst lush Eastern forests, Africa was a little off-putting, although I did return home with a magnificent mahogany brown tan.

The geology of the Keys is boring compared to the Rockies. In fact, the Keys didn't even exist until about 100,000 years ago and didn't resemble their present day selves until the end of the last Ice Age, the same time as when those massive boulders were deposited at David's Rock.

The Keys are coral formations, or more correctly parts of a massive coral formation that happened to poke their heads above water. As these islands evolved, wind, birds and water carried in botanical life and rich soil was formed from decayed organic material. Hurricanes and fires have depleted much of this soil. Humans have destroyed the rest, while rising seas as a consequence of global warming eventually will administer the *coup de grâce*.

Off-putting or not, we went back to Africa the following winter with anticipation, yards of mosquito netting, several hundred feet of garden hose, and Owen Owen, our new Irish amigo.

We used the netting to erect a sizable enclosure that the anoles got through anyway, and the hose to keep from having to ingratiate ourselves at Lazy Lakes.

Water pressure ranged from lousy to nonexistent everywhere in the Keys except Key West, which had its own pumping station, and got worse the further down the Keys one went from the mainland. Taking a shower at the campground was like standing under a watering can. Water pipes had to be run along the top of the ground because of the difficult-to-penetrate coral, and Hawk had discovered one such pipe the previous winter in the undergrowth along the road to Africa. It was about an inch in diameter and terminated at those two houses further down the road.

Hawk tapped into the pipe where it wouldn't be noticed, not that there would be anyone to do so, and was rewarded with a spurt of water. He installed a T-connector to which the garden hoses were attached. *Voila!* Africa had running water and, after Jack rigged a shower from a tree branch, a way to rinse off the salt from the lagoons. We took navy showers, first getting wet, soaping up and then rinsing off. It was divine.

Despite our warnings about the strength of the sub-tropical sun and the LSD he was doing with us , the fair-skinned Owen Owen copped a terrible sunburn after a couple of days of dawn-to-dusk exposure, his skin so lobster red that it bleached out his freckles. I drove him to the ER in Key West, supposing that such missions were my fate in life, where a nurse hydrated him, applied a salve and had a doctor write him a prescription for a painkiller. The doctor told us that most tourist visits to his ER were for bad sunburns, poisonwood smoke and Portuguese man-of-war stings.

We scavenged a dilapidated picnic table from the yard of one of the houses. We had carted the table back to Africa and screwed it back together before we noticed that among the graffiti skeeved into the top was

Gort Klaatu

which is a phrase from the science fiction classic, *The Day the Earth Stood Still*. Klaatu was the handsome humanoid alien protagonist played by Michael Rennie and Gort the robot that the damsel in distress, played by Patricia Neal, was told to prompt with the words "Klaatu barada nikto" if anything were to happen to Klaatu. Gort would then pulverize Earth. Not to spoil the plot, but Gort did not pulverize the Earth. We were thankful for that because Jack, Eldon and Owen Owen endlessly repeated the phrase to each other with great hilarity, chugging of beer, back slapping and high-fiving.

We lived inexpensively but large at Africa, our biggest expenses being beer and ice to keep the beer cold. We would buy fish at the docks in Key West and veggies from the farmers market in Homestead at the foot of the mainland.

A night on the town took the form of the short walk to Captain Tony's, a roadhouse at the Bow Channel Bridge opened, we were told, by a rum runner who smuggled in his cut-rate goods from Cuba during the Great Depression, a time when the Keys were first attracting serious attention from snowbirds and because Ernest Hemingway had made Key West his winter home. There was a bar, a few tables, a pool table and, inexplicably, a framed photograph of a mushroom cloud from a nuclear bomb blast on the wall between the men's and women's lavatories.

Missus Captain Tony had no idea why the photograph was there. It had come with the place when she and the now-dearly departed Captain bought it, but she though the guy sitting at the end of the bar might know.

Sam was a Conch, a native of the Keys and a fisherman who had lived his entire life on Sugarloaf. I asked him if he knew the provenance of the photograph.

"Dunno," he said. "Buy me a beer and I might remember."

I did but he didn't.

🏠

It was on a trip to Colorado that I met Hunter S. Thompson for the first time. The only other time we crossed paths was when he stopped by Africa with Teana, who had moved to Key West, and some of her townie friends, including a lass with whom the virginal Owen would trip the light fantastic for the first time.

Thompson, who had published the bestselling *Fear and Loathing in Las Vegas* the previous year, was gabbing with the Pitkin County district attorney in the bar of the

Jerome Hotel in Aspen when Zarnie and I stopped in for a cold one. Zarnie made introductions and promised Thompson -- for the umpteenth time, he told me later -- that he would vote for him in his unsuccessful if bodacious race for county sheriff on what Thompson called the Freak Ticket.

  The Freak Ticket was pure Thompson. He, like Rafe, had become radicalized after being rolled by the Chicago police at the 1968 Democratic National Convention, and was appalled at the extreme gentrification -- as in the influx of the billionaires who were pushing the millionaires up valley to Carbondale -- of the once sleepy backwater of Aspen after it became his adopted home.

  Thompson promised that if elected he would, among other things, hold a weekly Drug Tribunal on the lawn of the sheriff's department where dishonest drug dealers would be put in stocks. He said he also would change the name of Aspen to Fat City.

  I was a fan of Thompson as the progenitor of Gonzo journalism, typically first-person narratives written without even a veneer of objectivity, and had some writterly chops myself. For all I know, I might have been wearing a favorite T-shirt that evening. Across the front of the shirt was a Ralph Steadman pen-and-ink drawing from *Rolling Stone* magazine of the opening scene of *Fear and Loathing* of Thompson and his Samoan attorney streaking across the Nevada desert in a convertible with the words

> *He who makes a beast of himself*
> *rids the pain of being a man*

written below the drawing in the illustrator's inimitable scrawl.

Thompson had already proven himself to be incapable of sustaining his brilliance when he showed up at Africa. Being a gun nut, drug abuser and consumer of massive quantities of hard liquor had pretty much put him on the suicide track. Although it would be a fair number of years before he blew out what was left of his brains, it was sadly obvious that they were already on their way to being pickled.

He seemed to be even taller than he was in the bar at the Jerome, his height exaggerated by the broad-brimmed sun hat he still was wearing over aviator sunglasses although the sun had long set. He had on a many-pocketed khaki foreign correspondent jacket over an Hawaiian shirt, khaki pants, and was shod in canvas plimsolls. He held a cigarette holder in one hand, chain smoking pungent French Galois, and a plastic cup of

iced bourbon in the other. He only stopped jabbering --
about what I don't remember except that every fourth or
fifth word seemed to be "er," "uh" or "fuck" -- to take a
puff or a quaff.

  The conversation was one-sided, which I suppose
means that it really wasn't a conversation, although
Thompson did pause at one point and declared to no
one in particular, "Teana says uh you raise dairy goats.
I love goats uh milk wash 'em the fuck down with my
vitamins er . . . Let's get drunk."

"You already are drunk, you jerk," I muttered under
my breath. I was skeptical of the goats milk claim until I
later related the evening to Zarnie. Thompson, he said,
was a secret health nut who *did* drink goats milk to wash
down fists full of vitamins, the milk probably being the
only thing that kept his insides from imploding.

  Thompson retired periodically to an immense red
Cadillac rental convertible parked on the road side of
the dump to fetch ice from a bucket and a few fingers of
Wild Turkey from a quart bottle. This was his exclusive
domain, but he did gift us a case of gloriously cold Dos
Equis beer cosseted in two bags of ice that were melting
into the back seat of the Caddy. The front seat was as
far from the steering wheel as it would go, and there
was no question Thompson was the driver. Like the

Screamer, I could never picture him as a passenger and feared for those who were.

We all have secrets, but I was surprised when Thompson shrunk back in horror when Teana suggested that we skinny dip in the lagoon. The man who had so many crazy escapades, torn up countless hotel rooms, threatened to bury his attorney in the desert up to his neck, and bragged incessantly about pushing the proverbial envelope, was afraid of the water.

AFTERWORD

*"We were born before the wind, Also younger than the sun
Ere the bonnie boat was won as we sailed into the mystic"*

It's never a good sign when you long for a day to be over before it has begun, but that is how I felt as I threw a few things into the bus before saying goodbye to Kiln Farm. I had slept fitfully, was awakened by Percy's sunrise serenade as I had on my first night in the attic and many nights since, and then drifted in and out of sleep while musing during brief interludes of wakefulness on whether what I really wanted was to hang onto what I had and not have to face anything new.

That cop-out of a thought soon evaporated, and I padded downstairs to take a last shower. This was interrupted, much to my delight, when the rubber hose attached to the shower head came loose and soaked the bathroom in a farewell salute.

I breakfasted with Jack and Dadd, then walked around the garden, which was bejeweled with dew that refracted and amplified the light. A breeze gently rocked Caitlin's empty swing, while the only sounds were the hysterical *buckwheat-buckwheat* calls of a guineafowl hit squad in the upper garden. The row of white pine saplings we had planted as a windbreak between the side yard and lower garden during my first autumn at the farm had grown together. They were now nearly 15 feet tall. The scavenged restaurant kitchen door with the porthole that I had hung didn't close any more, and on this momentous day was covered with morning glories in full flower. The pine trees and opening made for a magical effect -- a verdure of evergreen green with a glimpse of the garden's many colors beyond.

I had few illusions about life when I moved to the farm and none when I left. I ended up there because I needed a place to stay while I sorted myself out. I loved my housemates, for the most part, but the years started to pile up. Then one day I realized it was time to move on. Getting away from cocaine, which had become the drug of choice for some of us later in the decade, had something to do with that, but so did seeing men digging holes in a field off the long driveway for perk tests, a prelude to construction of those townhouses.

Looking back on my decade at the farm from the perspective of encroaching dotage, two positive thoughts predominate: The farm let the magic come out. And the farm made me whole.

With the exception of Doctor Doc, who usually was ignored when he brought up anything going on beyond the kitchen table, we were an apolitical bunch. But the farm's founding fathers -- Doctor Duck and Davis -- had moved there on the cusp of the 1960s and 1970s, and Nam colored the times. Those colors were grays and blacks in stark contrast to the greens and earth tones of the farm.

The farm as we knew it would not have existed without the war and the social revolution of the late 1960s. That social revolution was bound to the war and the farm was inextricably bound to both. The farm was many things, but it was most of all a refuge, which was kind of counter intuitive since we were, for the most part, the products of comfy middle class suburbs. It was most especially a refuge for housemates who had survived the war. They drank, drugged and screwed to forget those times, and occasionally had nightmares about them. I know because The Island on Top of the World, as I came to call my attic lair, was over Doc's bedroom.

That name was not unlike Vi's description of her room across the hallway as The Room With the Hatch to the Universe. I didn't call my lair an island in conversations with friends, some of whom couldn't understand why I wanted to live at a place one of them derisively called Mildew Manor, but did so in my private thoughts. I would return from an expedition to New Park or Colorado or the Keys, climb the steps and open the door to the tinkling of the brass bells and the sight of that lovely floor, the barn siding ceiling and bookshelves, my houseplant jungle and the aroma of sandalwood incense. All the better if it was raining because the ratatat sound on the tin roof was like a lullaby.

The farm's magic didn't come out on its own, although that was the gauzy view of wannabes who believed it was a hippie Brigadoon and that every day was Flag Day.

I told the curious who would inquire about the magic that truths reached through explanation as opposed to experience are small truths. They were puzzled by my response. One guy who wanted to move in aspired to be like us, whatever that was. He never understood that you succeed by not trying to succeed.

As irreligious as most of us may have been, we were beneficiaries of a sort of God Job with the Almighty himself working the treadle of an invisible loom that wove the fabric of our collective lives. Is that over the top? I think not considering that save for one accident on a rain-slicked road and one attempt to flag down a train while standing on the tracks, none of us, except Doctor Duck, died let alone were badly hurt, while having the time of our lives. Our brushes with the law were nothing more than that. We took chances, but usually had enough sense to not repeat stupidly risky things. There was never an encore performance of my playing chicken with Doctor Duck as we bore down on each other on the state road. Concerns about Bigfoot getting blown up short-circuited a second batch of Jesus Grease. We didn't burn the house down, whether from candles or being inattentive to the dangers of the wood stove. We didn't cross back over that rope bridge, instead circumambulating back to my bus by hiking a few miles to where there was a safer crossing.

And we didn't play with guns. This is to be expected of young men who go off to war with a fondness for them, but come home with a very different perspective. Other than the rifle shot that put Bart out of his misery and another shot that killed a rabid red fox lurching through the back yard in the direction of little Caitlin, who of course was on her rope swing, there was never gun play of any kind.

I also have negative thoughts about the farm.

Beyond the imbalance between the men and women, there was a consequence of the times that reverberates even more loudly today: The sense of privilege among people who have done nothing to earn it. Most of us worked harder than we partied. We took our responsibilities to the critters and each other seriously. But the farm was a Promised Land for people like L.R., who were slackers long before that term entered the popular lexicon.

Then there were the drugs.

Marijuana and psychedelics were our totems early in the decade, and nothing particularly bad happened beyond getting a little banged up during volleyball games. Or occasionally walking into a wall. Pot and trips opened us up. They made us want to interact. They made us happy, sometimes so silly happy, that the scene around that octagonal table could have been from a Muppets movie free-for-all. Happiness is a relative concept, of course, but during the first few years at the farm, most of us were very happy people, as well as very much connected with the natural world -- the garden and fields on the other side of the kitchen door.

We were in a sense harbingers of the times early in the decade, while in later years later we became willing victims of the times as a darkness eventually descended in the form of cocaine.

It was a rare weekend when there weren't obscene quantities of cocaine gifted by visitors eager to pack our noses, and while not all of my housemates partook of coke, enough of us did and that profoundly changed the character of the farm. The passing of the mortar shell pipe was replaced by the passing of a mirror with cat's claw lines of white powder. Interactions were strained, and the scene around the table could have been from a Stephen King remake of *The Big Chill*. That natural world pretty much ceased to exist when we did coke.

We never locked the farmhouse. Nobody had any keys. But after the arrival of coke there were petty thefts and then more substantial stuff went missing like our first television set and even food from milk house freezers. We had to put hasps and padlocks on the doors.

When I moved to the farm, I was badly out of balance, which is to say strong of mind, but weak of body.

I was a book lover and experienced traveler who had dropped out of college, but knew more about things large and small than most graduates. I did not understand how much I was imbalanced until I found I was having trouble keeping up physically with some of my housemates. I apprenticed to Denny and Jack, and over a couple of years got back into shape while learning the finer points of the nail-bending trade.

My decade at the farm was very much a satori, and an idiosyncratic one to say the least. Swanee-Das, as Shell affectionately called me, was able to get a measure of his true self -- a nice guy who liked to give stuff to people, had a sizable intellect, a thirst for adventure, was lucky in lust but unlucky in love, and had a weakness for Colombian marching powder, although not an outright addiction to it.

Sooner or later, there is a price to pay for one's lifestyle if it is other than orthodox and not accepting of society's received truths, as our parents' generation was. Most of us eventually went straight, put away our tie-dyed shirts, and became less adventurous. That is what is commonly referred to as growing up, but I prefer to look at it through the other end of the telescope: We didn't so much grow up as succumb to the mechanistic gravity of the real world that compresses all but the roundest of pegs like Jack and Zarnie. Both of these dear friends are noble elements like platinum and gold. They resist combining with other elements and cannot be mixed or divided. They always will be square holes. About myself I'm not sure.

Neil Young ponders in the song "Hey Hey, My My (Into the Black)" whether it is better to burn out or fade away. Most of my housemates did neither. The farm was an incubator for living fuller lives. I can confirm that because I have remained in frequent touch with Jack and Zarnie, and in occasional touch with Hawk, Dadd, Teana and Vi, all of whom have lived the fullest of lives. (Jack has a German Shepherd and Teana an Australian Shepherd. Both are named Luna.) We all have taken the farm with us wherever we have gone, and whatever we have done. When I call my former housemates, I always identify myself as "Mullen from Kiln Farm." They do the same.

My travels seldom take me to New Park anymore, but when they do, I stop by the tavern and wander into what used to be the townie bar to see if a plaque I arranged to have engraved is still hanging there. It has a photo of Doctor Duck and the words:

> *For Many Years He Stood Here*
> *And Made New Park*
> *And The World A Better Place*

In the time-honored tradition of previous housemates, I left most of my stuff behind. This included a thousand or so record albums and the cabinets I made for them in the wood shop, as well as most of the books I had bought at used bookstores and flea markets on my travels, which had pretty much filled the shelves in my lair. I had devoured the histories and biographies, but most of the fiction, save for some science fiction, remained unread.

I did take some stuff, including buckets of cuttings from the ferns Pattie had planted, from the thicket under the front porch that I gave to a friend with whom I later fell in love. Many years on, they are thriving in the front yard of our house. The few other things I took away sit on a shelf across from my desk as I write these closing words: A copy of the *I Ching* and companion yarrow stalks Shell gifted me. Caitlin's "Y" toy building block. A clutch of Percy's tail feathers. The tattered remains of a faux pearl necktie from the first Flag Day party. Jack's copy of *The American Merchant Seaman's Manual* and my copy of *Be Here Now*. The five artist sketch books I had filled with my musings. That chorus-line photo of the crew about to board the Zymo for Colorado.

I carry a very tattered Lazy Lakes Left-Handers Club membership card in my wallet along with my Medicare and AARP cards. My back still sometimes aches from my dry dive from the ladder in the shed, while that massive draft horse of an hallucination from my first solo acid trip still occasionally inhabits my dreams.

Snakegrinder, meanwhile, has become a cult band 40 years after the release of their only album, which fetches big bucks on the Internet for collectors of obscure psychedelic-tinged 1970s music.

Mildew and run down-ness aside, there was an inherent beauty to Kiln Farm. I was fortunate to be able to live there for a mere fraction of its long history. The farm was very, very good to us and I suppose we were good to the farm, as well. If the barn could talk, I suppose it might have thanked us for saving it for a few more years.

Some of us discuss having a reunion, but I doubt that will happen. While we shared a special time, our lives are so different and many of us live so far apart. The closest thing to a reunion was a benefit concert a few years ago to help pay off Shell's medical expenses. She had a heart attack and called 911 before losing consciousness. Her windpipe was so tiny that paramedics couldn't get a breathing tube down her throat to revive her. She was declared brain dead, but lived for another three expensive, insurance-free months. Given her deep spirituality, I am sure she is having a fulfilling reincarnation whatever and wherever she may be.

I finally located Jena, Pattie's surviving daughter, and asked her whether she would like to have the jewelry case and other stuff her mother had entrusted to me. She said she would.

We met at a nature preserve about five miles from the farm where she works for a land trust organization. A picnic for trust interns had just finished, and I recognized Jena as she walked up a hill towards me. She has her mother's good looks, brown hair and long legs, but is taller. I would imagine that she also has the same penetrating blue eyes, but she was wearing sunglasses.

Like Pattie, Jena loves horses, and like Pattie is passionate about the environment. She blushed when I said her mother would be very proud of her.

Kiln Farm had amazing sights, smells and sounds.

We never were about performing, but Flag Day parties were high theater (pun intended). As I looked out across the lawn on party weekends at the masses surging to and fro, the light from the late afternoon sun giving this grandly sublime scene a Dionysian quality, it was obvious we had created a monster -- albeit a beneficent monster -- at least for the first few years.

There was the sweet aroma of marijuana plants curing in the shed loft. The stench of the chicken coop. Shell's fresh-baked banana bread. Dr. Bronner's Peppermint Shampoo in the bathroom. Dadd's chicken with his secret sauce barbecuing on the grill. The potpourri simmering in the kettle atop the wood stove. Pattie's mulberry and rhubarb pie. Lobelia's breathy attar of oats and hay.

More deafeningly loud rock concerts than I can count notwithstanding, I have always had an acute sense of hearing, and was able to tune into the sounds the farm made: Pops. Booms. Cracks. Rattles. Whistles. Groans. The wind chimes on the front porch. Gunshot-like sounds in the autumn when black walnuts fell from the tree little Caitlin swung under onto the chicken coop roof. The click-click of tree branches on the upper story windows in the winter. Bart woofing at the moon. And a faint noise sounding like a faraway chorus of laughter.

We joked that the farm was haunted by good ghosts. That the forebears who lived and died there long before we barged onto the scene, must have been a mellow lot. It didn't seem likely an apparition of Old Man Van der Killen would emerge from a wall wielding a knife, peg-leg across a room and make for one of our necks. Perhaps that chorus was the whole bunch of them laughing over how barking mad we were.

THE TRIBE TODAY

Ali: Unknown
Bess: Died of ovarian cancer
Bigfoot: Died of heart attack
Bix: Contractor
Caitlin: Died in car crash
Callie: Tai chi instructor
Dadd: Gentleman farmer
Dan: Died of lung cancer
Davis: Unknown
Denny: Beekeeper, reformed alcoholic
Doctor Doc: Orchid specialist
Doctor Duck: Died of liver failure
Edward: Run over by train
Hawk: Retired, tinkerer
Jack: Trucker
Jane: Mother
Jena: Environmentalist
Pattie: Died in car crash
Shaun: Writer
Shell: Died of heart attack complications
Teana: Teacher, gardener
Vi: Horse whisperer
Zarnie: Solar energy pioneer

CODA: BROKEDOWN PALACE

Fare you well, my honey
Fare you well my only true one
All the birds that were singing
Are flown, except you alone

Don't want to leave this broke down palace
On my hands and my knees, I will roll, roll, roll
Make myself a bed by the waterside
In my time, in my time, I will roll, roll, roll

In a bed, in a bed, by the waterside
I will lay my head
Listen to the river sing sweet songs
To rock my soul

River going to tame me, sing sweet and sleepy
Sing me sweet and sleepy all the way back home
It's a far gone lullaby, sung many years ago
Mama, mama many worlds I've come since I first left home

Goin' home, goin' home
By the waterside I will lay my bones
Listen to the river sing sweet songs
To rock my soul

Going to plant a weeping willow
By the bank's green edge it will grow, grow, grow
Sing a lullaby beside the water
Lovers come and go, the river roll, roll, roll

Fare you well, fare you well
I love you more than words can tell
Listen to the river sing sweet songs
To rock my soul

ABOUT THE AUTHOR

Shaun D. Mullen has written about the wars in Vietnam, Iraq and Afghanistan, the O.J. Simpson trials, Clinton impeachment circus, War on Terror, and 10 presidential campaigns during five decades as a reporter, editor and blogger. His work as an investigative editor was nominated for five Pulitzer Prizes, while he mentored reporters who went on to be the best in the newspaper and television business, including several who won Pulitzer Prizes. He is the author of *The Bottom of the Fox: A True Story of Love, Devotion & Cold-Blooded Murder*.

The author may be contact at ahouseintheland@gmail.com

To comment on the book and for updates, go to theresahouseintheland.blogspot.com

ABOUT THE ARTIST

Anja Gudic is an award-winning New York City-based artist and illustrator whose work appears in *Family Circle* magazine and on its website, and in other publications.

Visit her website at www.planetaillustration.com

Made in the USA
Middletown, DE
02 January 2017